MW01281809

THE BLOCKBUSTER COMPLEX

Also By Thomas Whiteside

THE BLOCKBUSTER COMPLEX

Conglomerates, Show Business, and Book Publishing

THOMAS WHITESIDE

WESLEYAN UNIVERSITY PRESS
MIDDLETOWN, CONNECTICUT

Nearly all of the text of this book appeared originally
in *The New Yorker*.

Library of Congress Cataloging in Publication Data
Whiteside, Thomas.
  The blockbuster complex.
   "Nearly all of the text of this book appeared originally
   in the New Yorker."—Verso t.p.
  Includes index.
  1. Publishers and publishing—United States.
I. Title.
Z471.W47 07.5'0973   81-7453
ISBN 0-8195-5057-4   AACR2

DISTRIBUTED FOR WESLEYAN UNIVERSITY PRESS
BY COLUMBIA UNIVERSITY PRESS
136 SOUTH BROADWAY, IRVINGTON, NY 10533

MANUFACTURED IN THE UNITED STATES OF AMERICA

FIRST EDITION

Designed by Sidney Feinberg

310083

To William Shawn

Contents

THE BLOCKBUSTER COMPLEX

CHAPTER 1

Drastic Changes

BERNARD BARUCH is supposed to have remarked once that when the financial news gets onto the front page the time has come for people to watch out. Perhaps the remark could now be revised to apply to the American book-publishing business. As late as the nineteen-fifties, trade-book publishing—that is, the publishing of books of general interest, as distinct from textbooks and other specialized works—was believed to offer its practitioners a rather select and gentlemanly way of life. It may not have been considered a particularly profitable business, or a notably efficient one, but it was a business in which publishers and editors could feel sustained not only by their love of books but also by their sense of professional independence, arising from the fact that most publishing houses were independently owned and run, and by a diversity of relatively stable relationships with authors, agents, and booksellers.

Since the early nineteen-sixties, however, trade-book publishing has been subjected to some startling changes, which have tended to affect these attitudes and relationships, and even in some ways to affect the course of writing itself. The clearest manifestations of drastic change involve the ownership of particular houses. There has been a seemingly relentless trend toward concentrating the ownership of individual publishing houses into ever-larger corporate organizations. Privately owned publishing companies have been converted into publicly held corporations, and often these corporations have, in turn, been absorbed into huge conglomerate organizations. As part of this trend, paperback publishing houses have become merged with hardcover houses, and now nearly all the leading publishers of both kinds of books are owned by conglomerates.

In the past twenty years or so, the hardcover trade-book houses of Alfred A. Knopf and Pantheon Books were taken over by Random House, and Random House was acquired by RCA. Random House then acquired the formerly independent paperback publishing company Ballantine Books. And then RCA sold Random House to Newhouse Publications, which owns the Newhouse newspaper chain. In the last four years, Dell Publishing, one of the principal mass-market-paperback houses, was acquired by Doubleday & Company, the largest trade-book publisher in the country, which had previously acquired, among other enterprises, the Literary Guild, the nation's second-largest book club. Another mass-market-paperback publisher, Fawcett Publications, was acquired by CBS, which had already acquired yet another mass-market-paperback house, Popular Library, and the hardcover house Holt, Rinehart & Winston. The hardcover house Bobbs-Merrill was acquired by the International Telephone & Telegraph Corporation. Pocket Books, a leading paperback publisher, was acquired, as part of the hardcover house Simon & Schuster, by the conglomerate Gulf & Western, which also owned Paramount Pictures. G. P. Putnam's Sons, which had acquired the trade-book house of Coward, McCann & Geoghegan and the paperback publisher Berkley Books, was acquired by MCA, which had earlier acquired Universal

Pictures. The hardcover house Viking Press became a part of Penguin Books, which, in turn, was owned by a conglomerate known as the Pearson-Longman group. Bantam Books, another of the leading paperback publishers, wound up under the control of Bertelsmann Verlag, of Germany, probably the largest publishing concern in the world. The hardcover house E. P. Dutton was acquired by the Dutch publishing complex Elsevier. Another hardcover house, Little, Brown & Company, was acquired by Time, Inc., which subsequently acquired the largest existing book club, the Book-of-the-Month Club. And this is only a partial listing of corporate mergers in the publishing business in the recent past.

In keeping with the scale of these corporate consolidations, many other aspects of the book-publishing business appear to have grown dramatically. Things just seem to keep getting bigger and bigger. Big deals are everywhere. A payment of a million dollars for paperback rights to a single book has become commonplace, and in one instance more than three times that sum was realized for the rights to a work of popular fiction. Such transactions are front-page news, and the comings and goings of popular authors, their working lives, their wealth, their marriages, divorces, and liaisons, their intramural squabbles, and their off-the-cuff opinions on everything are the subject of such an incessant stream of publicity that in a sense such authors have been invested with the glamour once reserved for movie stars. Popular authors, agents, packagers—all these are movers and shakers in the new age of book publishing.

While this trend toward mergers did not begin in the nineteen-sixties—acquisitions of smaller publishers by bigger publishers had been taking place piecemeal since the start of the century, and even earlier—it was in 1960 that it received its first big impetus: the absorption of Alfred A. Knopf into Random House, which set the tone for what happened later. As with many subsequent mergers, prime considerations in bringing about this one were the age of the founder and active head of the acquired company and his decision to take steps to settle his personal estate and assure his company's continued stability. Knopf, which had been founded forty-five years previously, was considered the most distinguished book house in America—the publisher of works by such authors as W. H. Hudson, Thomas Mann, André Gide, Albert Camus, T. S. Eliot, Ezra Pound, H. L. Mencken, Katherine Mansfield, E. M. Forster, Robert Graves, and Jean-Paul Sartre. By 1959, the founder and his son, Alfred Knopf, Jr., who was a vice-president at Knopf, had developed such difficulties in their relationship that Alfred, Jr., decided to leave the firm and, together with Simon Michael Bessie, who had been editor-in-chief of Harper & Bros., and Hiram Haydn, who had been editor-in-chief of Random House, he formed a new publishing house, Atheneum. The possibility that this move would raise uncertainties concerning the eventual family succession at Knopf—Blanche Knopf, the wife of the senior Knopf, ran the company with her husband, and she, too, was getting on in years—was not lost on Bennett Cerf, the president of Random House, and a great professional and personal admirer of Knopf.

Cerf and his partner, Donald Klopfer, had made a great success of Random House, which they founded together in the mid-twenties. Random House had its origin in the purchase, in 1925, of the Modern Library imprint from Horace Liveright, of Boni & Liveright—a firm that had come upon hard times, mostly as a result of inattentive management. Under Cerf and Klopfer, the Modern Library series, which was probably the greatest asset of Boni & Liveright, began to sell much better than previously, and in 1927 Cerf and Klopfer issued their first book—a luxury edition of Melville's *Benito Cereno*. It was followed, a year later, by luxury editions of *Candide* (illustrated by Rockwell Kent, this was the first book brought out under the new imprint of Random House) and *The Divine Comedy.* In non-luxury editions, all these soon became part of an expanded Modern Library series—the reasonably priced set of classic works that, like the paperback Penguin series in England, is affectionately remembered by so many readers for the part it played in developing a lifetime enjoyment of books.

Within a few years, Random House branched out from the publication of new editions of the classics, and developed a list that included such authors as James Joyce, Eugene O'Neill, Gertrude Stein, William Faulkner, W. H. Auden, and Robert Penn Warren. The American edition of *Ulysses* was the first important trade book by a living author that Random House published, and Cerf and Klopfer managed to achieve its American publication by devising a legal stratagem for challenging the United States Customs Service, which had declared the work obscene and therefore subject to confiscation—a challenge that resulted in the famous obscenity trial in which Judge John M. Woolsey found *Ulysses* to be not obscene but a work of artistic merit. As for Cerf himself, the publisher of *Ulysses* was not above becoming, on the side, the author of joke books, a newspaper humor columnist, and a well-known panel member of the TV quiz show "What's My Line?"—in general, a literary wheeler-dealer with a finger in every piece of the mass-media pie.

While Cerf and Klopfer for practical purposes owned and completely controlled Random House between them, they came to realize in the late nineteen-fifties that the company's very success could pose certain financial problems for them and for the operation of the company itself. Both men were of advanced middle age, and they now had to face the fact that when, eventually, one of them died there was no telling precisely what difficulties might be involved in putting a value on the company for tax purposes—especially since much of the profit over the years had been plowed back into the business for future expansion. One way in which the Internal Revenue Service ordinarily gauged the value of a corporation for estate-tax purposes was by the current price of its stock on the market, but since Random House was privately owned that yardstick was lacking. There was the possibility that when one of them died, the government might place such a high value on the estate that the surviving partner, if he wanted to buy the deceased partner's share of the company, might not be able to afford it. In fact, the valuation might turn out to be so high that the widow of the deceased partner might be hard pressed to raise enough cash just to pay the estate tax. And that situation would put pressure on her and any other heirs to sell their interest in the company to a third party.

To avert such difficulties, the partners drew up a contract under which the survivor could buy the deceased partner's share for the fixed sum of half a million dollars—thereby establishing a value for the company which it was hoped would be acceptable to government estate examiners. Going one step further toward establishing the value of the Random House estate—and, at the same time, setting the stage for the expansion of the company—Cerf and Klopfer consulted Charles Allen, the head of the big investment-banking organization of Allen & Company, about the possibility of a public stock issue for Random House. Allen thought that was a good idea, and in October of 1959 thirty per cent of Cerf's and Klopfer's stock was offered for sale through Allen & Company. It was quickly snapped up on Wall Street.

Shortly thereafter, Cerf approached Alfred Knopf and suggested that a merger between Random House and Knopf would insure managerial continuity in the house of Knopf—Alfred and Blanche Knopf would continue to run the com-

pany as before, with a guarantee of editorial autonomy—
and for as long as Alfred Knopf was at the helm the merger
would relieve him of the burden of handling certain business
details. He agreed to this arrangement, and in the spring of
1960 his company became part of Random House, with
Alfred and Blanche Knopf being recompensed in cash and
Random House stock.

Wall Street had already begun to take an interest in publishing companies, and this news spurred that interest. The
stock market was booming, and before long several other
privately owned book-publishing companies followed the
lead of Random House in putting substantial blocks of their
stock up for sale. The stock of Random House itself had
gone on the market at eleven dollars and twenty-five cents
a share, and in twenty-four hours it had risen to fourteen
dollars. In a series of tape-recorded reminiscences elicited
during interviews by Mary R. Hawkins, of the Columbia
University Oral History Collection, which formed the basis
for a book that Random House published in 1977, some six
years after Cerf's death, under the title *At Random*, Cerf
remarked of the period immediately after his company went
public, "From then on, we were publishing with one eye
and watching our stock with the other. Then several other
firms went public, and suddenly the prices of all these unseasoned stocks began to escalate. It was frightening because they went up without rhyme or reason. In one week,
for instance, Random House stock went up by more than
the price at which we had issued it."

At the end of the summer of 1961, Random House stock
went on the New York Stock Exchange for trading, but it
didn't prosper immediately; a recession had set in that year,
and though the economy as a whole recovered rather
quickly, it was not until the mid-nineteen-sixties that Random House stock made a recovery. By then, various big
electronics companies had become interested in the pub-

lishing business. "Synergy" had become the word to use in discussions of corporate mergers involving the electronics industry. The boom in the data-processing business that accompanied the domestic social-welfare and aid-to-education programs of Lyndon Johnson's Presidency led many of the leaders of big electronics companies to speculate that there was tremendous potential in the arranging of corporate marriages through which the production of books would be integrated into, for example, electronically oriented systems for the public schools. What the leaders saw was a world of computerized teaching machines, readout screens, and pupil instruction by instrumented input-and-feedback schemes, with a great range of textbooks and other works controlled by the publishing industry as the "software" to be fed into this electronic instructional maw. With such possibilities in mind, representatives of RCA sounded out Cerf and Klopfer about the chances of RCA's acquiring Random House, with not only its impressive list of trade books but also the Modern Library, the great Knopf list of authors, and a profitable line of juvenile books and elementary- and high-school textbooks. Through the investment-banking firms of Lazard Frères and Lehman Brothers, a merger was arranged, and in May of 1966, in return for nearly thirty-eight million dollars, Random House became part of RCA. In a statement announcing the sale, Cerf said that the agreement reflected "our conviction that publishing and electronics are natural partners for the incredible expansion immediately ahead for every phase of education in our country."

This merger dramatized a marked trend toward book-publishing software acquisitions by big communications companies—though the acquisition of Bobbs-Merrill by I.T.&T., which had taken place eight years earlier, was the actual precursor. Only a year after the Random House-RCA merger, CBS acquired Holt, Rinehart & Winston, and it went on to acquire the hardcover house Praeger Publishers, as well as Popular Library and Fawcett. The Xerox Corporation, which, for different reasons, also went into the computer business, acquired the major textbook-publishing house of Ginn & Company and the R. R. Bowker Company, the publisher of various yearbooks and reference works for the publishing industry and of the principal journal of the book-publishing trade itself, *Publishers Weekly.*

As it happens, the big corporations' expectations of a future in which banks of electronic teaching machines tended by storage-and-retrieval systems would produce a new generation of plugged-in, electronically fedback pupils have not been rewarded. The government's preoccupation with the Vietnam War put a damper on many of the big federal aid-to-education programs that had been contemplated, and the student revolt against the war extended to almost the entire structure of higher education, throwing into disarray the accepted notions about the use of the standard textbooks and other software assets of the book-publishing companies that large corporations had acquired. All in all, during the conglomerate-merger boom the concept of the electronic classroom remained just a concept. The editor-in-chief of a well-known trade-book house remarked, "The whole thing, everybody realized later, was something of a joke. The technology involved never did stand up—all those supposedly sophisticated versions of teaching machines turned out to be pretty primitive, and they still haven't really worked, even though we're now hearing a new round of promises about all the benefits that advances in microcircuitry and so on can bring to education. And one of the ironies is that the printed book, which hasn't changed substantially in five hundred years, has been discovered after all to be a remarkably cheap way of storing and retrieving knowledge." As for RCA's attempt to become a leading force in the manufacture of computer "mainframe" hardware, that failed, too, at great financial loss to RCA. And the same misfortune befell the computer-business aspirations of Xerox, although the company still turns out software and some hardware components. But if the vision of the electronic classroom and its accompanying literary software remained somewhat chimerical, the corporate mergers that had taken place were accomplished fact. And the over-all competitive strivings of the various conglomerates that owned publishing companies provided a momentum for the continuation right through the sixties and seventies of the practice of acquiring publishing companies and absorbing them into larger and larger corporate organizations. At present, apart from some large publishing companies that have become conglomerate-like organizations in themselves—McGraw-Hill, Doubleday, Harper & Row, Harcourt Brace Jovanovich—the number of major independent hardcover book publishers that have not succumbed to the corporate-merger wave can be counted on the fingers of one hand: W. W. Norton; Farrar, Straus & Giroux; Houghton Mifflin; Scribners; and Crown. Of the ten largest trade publishers in the country, only three—Macmillan, Houghton Mifflin, and Crown—are not conglomerate-owned. And only a last-minute breakdown in negotiations prevented Macmillan from being acquired by ABC in the fall of 1979.

All this has caused uneasiness in the literary community; for example, within the last several years the Authors Guild, which represents the interests of more than five thousand professional writers in this country, has sent a series of communications to the Federal Trade Commission, the Department of Justice, and the Judiciary Committees of both houses of Congress asserting that the trend toward concentration and conglomeration in various kinds of book publishing has been going beyond the limits of fair competition as defined in the Clayton Anti-Trust Act; that it threatens the survival of the remaining independently owned companies; that it is contrary to the " 'uninhibited marketplace of ideas' guaranteed by the First Amendment;" and that for many authors of artistically meritorious works lacking immediate commercial appeal it jeopardizes or diminishes their bargaining power with publishers and their opportunity to be published.

The response of the Association of American Publishers, the book industry's national trade association, whose more than three hundred member companies account for about eighty-five per cent of all books published in the United States, was summed up in December of 1978 by Townsend Hoopes, its president, at a public seminar on "Concentration in the Media," which was conducted in Washington by the Federal Trade Commission. Characterizing the position of the Authors Guild as "extreme" and its views as "a distorted picture of reality," Hoopes declared that, contrary to implications by the Authors Guild that "the nation is on the brink of a social or cultural catastrophe owing to merger activity and alleged overconcentration in book publishing," the publishing industry was in fact "amazingly diverse, flexible, and open." Mergers had not reduced the number of competitive companies in publishing, he said, and "concentration, per se, has been a modest development." He went on to say that "good books have never been in more plentiful supply and have never reflected greater diversity of subject matter or treatment" and that "authors have never been more numerous or better rewarded." Hoopes maintained that the number of American publishing companies, far from decreasing, had actually increased by more than thirty per cent during the past twenty years, and that even after failures and mergers in the industry were taken into account, the number was continuing to increase at a steady rate of two or three per cent a year. To illustrate what he termed the open nature of the publishing market,

Hoopes pointed out that a hundred and seventy-three companies that had not existed before 1971 published more than four thousand new titles in 1976, most of them hardcover trade books. This represented some ten per cent of the new book titles published that year. In sum, according to Hoopes, the book industry was healthy and stable, in terms of both its structure and the variety of works being published.

The situation out of which such strongly divergent views have arisen is a highly complex one, and involves the growth and interplay of a number of forces, among which the merger trend might be considered in the light not only of cause but of effect, and might also be seen as part of a larger web of economic circumstances. As to direct cause and effect, the original impetus for many of the mergers of publishing houses in the nineteen-sixties was the dilemma of the aging proprietors of family-owned houses who were trying to settle their personal estates and put their corporate affairs in order—and, of course, to make handsome capital gains on the deal as well. The moment these houses went public—which sometimes happened before any major merger actually took place—their owners and managers found that although they still controlled the companies, their control and the kind of decisions they had been used to making on a peremptory basis were likely to be tempered by considerations they had never before had to reckon with. A sense of the problem is conveyed in Bennett Cerf's *At Random*. In discussing the decision he and Klopfer made in 1959 to issue Random House stock to the public, Cerf observed:

> This marked a big change, since the minute you go public, outsiders own some of your stock and you've got to make periodic reports to them. You owe your investors dividends and profits. Instead of working for yourself and doing what you damn please, willing to risk a loss on something you want to

do, if you're any kind of honest man, you feel a real responsibility to your stockholders.

If a publisher's predilection for "working for yourself and doing what you damn please" was modified by his company's going public, it was likely to be reined in even more tightly when the company was acquired by a larger company or a conglomerate. For the most part, the restraint involved was a natural response to a new and more complex corporate and financial environment. In many cases, the mere fact that a privately owned publishing house went public meant an initial net gain in efficiency and productivity, because the whole process of putting the owner's affairs in order and determining the market worth of his company inevitably involved detailed disclosure and examination of the company's financial records, for the purpose of complying with the requirements of the Securities and Exchange Commission for stock offerings, and of giving potential stockholders a fair picture of the company's operations, marketing practices, and prospects. Most of the publishing houses whose owners were contemplating public stock issues or discussing mergers had never been subjected to such scrutiny, and the examinations frequently brought to light deficiencies in business and financial-management practices, many of which were hallowed by book-publishing tradition and had gone uncorrected through managerial inertia.

The book-publishing business was indeed riddled with inefficiency: often sluggish management, agonizingly slow editorial and printing processes, creaky and ill-coördinated systems of book distribution and sales, skimpy advertising budgets, and—a most important factor during economic ups and downs—an inadequate system of financing, which prevented many publishers from undertaking major long-range editorial projects that they knew were necessary to their companies' future well-being. With perhaps a few exceptions, the trade-book business was not a particularly high-profit industry, and, furthermore, the profits of a given publisher tended to vary greatly from one year to another, depending on his success or failure in selling his seasonal lists of books. Also, inflation was increasing the cost of materials and printing, and in particular the cost of maintaining a staff of salesmen on the road, whose responsibility it was to deal with jobbers, other wholesalers, and retail bookstores throughout the country. Keeping up with these problems and maintaining the degree of financial liquidity necessary to cope with the peculiar fluctuations of the business were becoming increasingly difficult for publishers, and their often urgent cash-flow problems—for example, in financing a projected series of books involving large outlays of money—couldn't always be resolved by simple recourse to the banks, because bankers tended to regard a book project or an author's manuscript as dubious and shadowy stuff until it was declared otherwise by the ringing of cash registers in bookstores.

The publishers who were willing to have their companies merged into larger companies had to take still another look at their business inadequacies. For some, that meant having to accommodate such practices of the modern corporate world as efficient accounting systems, long-range planning, and the elimination of waste and the unnecessary duplication of services. After the mergers took place, the principal visible changes in the publishing companies' day-to-day operation were fairly straightforward improvements in efficiency: the combining of sales forces with the acquiring company, centralized book-warehousing systems, and central, computerized inventory and other accounting-control systems. If this efficiency was achieved at the cost of some managerial independence in making certain major business decisions, and of sensing the hovering presence, in either the foreground or the background, of the acquiring company's accountants or newly established staff committees reporting to the accountants, the changes at least relieved those in charge of the acquired company of many of their former financial worries. They now had the benefit of being able to draw on substantial funds for expansion and for big editorial projects, and of having enough flexibility to acquire, through competitive or preëmptive bidding, the rights to high-priced works that as independent publishers they might not have been able to finance themselves. They had the benefit of stabilizing their cash flow over difficult periods—most notably, over the often lengthy interval between the time when a decision was made to go ahead with a particular book project and the time when the finished book was actually sold in bookstores. One general effect was a net competitive gain for those trade-book publishers who decided to merge into larger corporate entities. In 1977, Ronald Busch, then the president of Ballantine Books (which was taken under the RCA-Random House corporate umbrella in 1973), was quoted in *Publishers Weekly* as saying, "With all the conglomerate money in publishing today, it's like playing Monopoly. If we had to use our own resources, we'd think twice about bidding as much as we do. . . . But with a parent or a conglomerate that has annual sales of two billion dollars and up, with two or three million shareholders, what is the risk? What's the diminution of stockholder dividends if you are wrong? A mil in most cases." Not surprisingly, those independent publishers who resisted the temptation to be acquired began to encounter difficulties in maintaining or improving their position in the market, since that market was increasingly influenced by the larger amounts that houses backed by conglomerates could bid for books by popular writers. In sum, the mergers tended to increase the pressures on the remaining independent publishers to go along with the trend, in order to maintain their position in the book market. Merger begat merger, and since the nineteen-sixties the trend has continued.

CHAPTER 2

The Author-Tour
Business

ONE CHANGE in the book business that has
been intimately connected with the merger trend has to do
with the relation of hardcover books to paperbacks—particularly to mass-market paperbacks. Until the nineteen-
sixties, hardcover publishers controlled most literary rights.
In return for the advances on royalties which they offered
their authors, they retained, through their contracts with
the authors, not only the domestic rights to hardcover publication of individual works but also nearly all subsidiary
rights, including book-club and paperback rights, but usually not including movie rights and foreign sales. Usually,
the publishers retained half the proceeds of the sale of subsidiary rights. By the nineteen-sixties, however, the control
that hardcover publishers exercised over these rights was
being loosened. For one thing, the mass-market-paperback
business was becoming increasingly prosperous, and competition for the reprint rights to best-selling hardcover novels and other works was steadily growing, with progressively bigger advances being paid. For another, the authors
of popular works—or their agents—began to balk at the
hardcover houses' control over subsidiary rights, and, in
the area of best-sellers, began insisting that they have a far

greater say than they had had in the past. Agents now insisted on contracts in which they had increased negotiating power concerning various subsidiary rights. In the case of paperback rights, for example, some agents began to demand, and get, more than fifty per cent of the proceeds for their writers. And the amounts being demanded of and paid by paperback houses for the rights to books that looked like best-sellers kept rising. So did the advances being paid by hardcover houses for works that the publishers calculated might make the best-seller lists.

The steady growth that was taking place in the paperback market, combined with the loosening of the traditional control by hardcover houses over subsidiary rights, helped persuade a number of hardcover publishers to involve themselves directly in paperback publishing. Random House acquired Ballantine; G. P. Putnam's acquired Berkley Books; Harcourt Brace Jovanovich acquired Pyramid Books; and Pocket Books, which in the early part of its history had been closely affiliated with Simon & Schuster but had later evolved into an independent company, was merged with its old affiliate in 1970, and both were acquired in 1975 by Gulf & Western. The hardcover publishers calculated that by adding a paperback branch to their corporate organizations they could smooth out some of the ups and downs of their business, making up on the swings what they might lose on the roundabouts. Also, such dual ownership would give them increased flexibility for maneuvering in the market, since they would be free to make deals to publish both the hardcover and the paperback editions of particular books and would thus be in a position to attract certain authors to their lists by guaranteeing them favorable terms on both hardcover and paperback publication. As for the paperback publishers who decided to merge with corporations having hardcover houses, they could envision, besides the possible capital gains involved and the benefits of access to large cash reserves for future operations, such advantages as having a competitive edge through access to inside information on impending acquisitions by the hardcover branch of the corporation. All in all, to both participants the arrangement offered the prospect of increasing their share of the market and their influence in the book business as a whole. However the envisioned advantages may have actually worked out in specific mergers, the result of this further kind of consolidation has been that few of the major hardcover houses are now without a paperback branch, and people in the few remaining independent, unmerged, unconglomerated hardcover houses complain that doing business without having a paperback branch tends to place them at a competitive disadvantage.

Just as the publishing mergers appear to have stimulated the process of absorption of independent book houses into ever-larger corporate organizations, so the actual sums being offered for mass-market-paperback reprint rights to actual or potential best-sellers have mounted rapidly on their own momentum: one deal big enough to set the publishing community abuzz with excitement merely serves to trigger even bigger deals. The upshot is that the entire economy of trade-book publishing seems to have become focussed on the pursuit of "the big book"—the so-called blockbuster. A few examples of the prices that have been paid for paperback rights to best-sellers—fiction or nonfiction—indicate how the bidding has gone in a dozen or so years. In 1968, Putnam sold Fawcett the paperback rights to Mario Puzo's *The Godfather* for four hundred and ten thousand dollars. In 1972, Harper & Row sold Avon the paperback rights to *I'm O.K.—You're O.K.*, a lay guide to self-analysis, by Dr. Thomas A. Harris, for a million dollars, which was then the highest price in publishing history for paperback rights. Just a month later, Avon paid $1,100,000 to Macmillan for the rights to Richard Bach's *Jonathan*

Livingston Seagull. In 1974, Simon & Schuster, even before publishing its hardcover edition of Bob Woodward and Carl Bernstein's *All the President's Men* (the writers had received an advance of sixty thousand dollars), sold Warner Books the paperback rights for a million dollars. In 1975, Random House sold Bantam Books the rights to E. L. Doctorow's *Ragtime* for $1,850,000. In 1976, Avon paid Simon & Schuster $1,550,000 for the rights to Woodward and Bernstein's *The Final Days* and Harper & Row $1,900,000 for the rights to Colleen McCullough's novel *The Thorn Birds.* In 1978, Fawcett paid Harper & Row $2,250,000 for the rights to *Linda Goodman's Love Signs,* and in the same year New American Library paid Putnam $2,550,000 for the rights to Mario Puzo's *Fools Die*—a sum that included the conversion of the reprint rights to *The Godfather,* which had by then sold thirteen million paperback copies in the Fawcett edition. In 1979, Dell paid Doubleday a million dollars for the paperback rights to Thomas Thompson's *Serpentine;* Bantam Books paid Random House $1,500,000 for the rights to William Styron's *Sophie's Choice;* New American Library paid three million dollars for the rights to both Robin Cook's *Sphinx* and his next book, *Brain,* which Putnam was to publish in February of 1981. And in September of 1979 that figure was topped by a little less than a quarter of a million dollars, when Crown sold Bantam the paperback rights to a single novel, Judith Krantz's *Princess Daisy,* for $3,208,875. Under such circumstances, the sale of paperback rights for, say, half a million dollars hardly creates more than a ripple of interest in the trade. "I've heard people say, 'You mean you only got *six hundred thousand* for the paperback rights to that book?'" an agent with West Coast connections told me. Another man who has been involved in many paperback-rights deals observed, "This is a golden time for authors," and Oscar Dystel, former chairman of the board of Bantam Books, remarked to me, "You won't find a lot of these writers sitting in attics these days. You'll find them sitting in their big houses on their big estates. Or in their Rolls-Royces."

The erosion of the control traditionally held by hardcover houses, and the correspondingly increased dominance of the paperback end of the publishing business, has tended to make hardcover publishers more dependent than ever on revenues from the sale or lease of whatever subsidiary rights—primarily paperback rights—they have retained. For hardcover publishers, these revenues tend to vary greatly from one period to another, but their importance is such that, in the publishers' annual financial statement, they often constitute the difference between profit and loss. At the 1978 Federal Trade Commission seminar, Winthrop Knowlton, the chairman and chief executive officer of Harper & Row, which is the tenth-largest book publisher in the country, said that in 1977 Harper & Row's trade-book department had earned six hundred thousand dollars, after taxes, from hardcover sales and eight hundred thousand dollars from subsidiary rights. Knowlton's statement conveyed the clear implication that if the subsidiary-rights income of Harper & Row's trade-book department had fallen off substantially that year, the company's trade-book business as a whole would have been operating at a loss. And Roger W. Straus, Jr., the president of Farrar, Straus & Giroux, and the most vocal spokesman concerning the independent publishers' situation, has declared that his company "would be destitute without subsidiary-rights income."

To render this less than stable situation even more unstable, as the prices obtained by hardcover publishers from paperback houses for reprint rights keep rising, the competition among hardcover publishers to sell off the subsidiary rights to big books intensifies, and that means that the publishers concentrate their attention more and more on seeking out and promoting potential best-sellers. This concentration on the blockbuster is reinforced by other developments that have been occurring in the industry—among them the growth of large chains of retail bookstores, the strong rivalry of paperback publishers for rack space in retail outlets, the computerization of inventory and warehousing systems, the arrival on the scene of a new breed of big-time literary agent, the influence of television talk shows that regularly feature authors as guests, the control by entertainment conglomerates of hardcover and paperback publishing companies as well as motion-picture companies and the like, and the increasingly active involvement of Hollywood in the business of book publishing itself.

These diverse forces have contributed greatly to the grinding out of products by the huge conglomerate communications-entertainment economic engine. And at the same time the scale and complexity of this engine, or system, has exerted an extremely powerful influence on the condition of its components. For example, some components—among them the hardcover-book business—that were previously thought of as differing structurally and functionally have in various ways been standardized, and equipped with mutually compatible or interchangeable features, in the interests of accommodating them to the requirements of the machine as a whole. In this sense, the trade-book business seems on the way to becoming nothing more than the component of the conglomerate communications-entertainment complex which happens to deal primarily with publishing books. Just how far-reaching that complex is can be seen in the fact that Harcourt Brace Jovanovich has made itself the owner of several marine-life recreation exhibitions in this country, including Sea World, in Florida, which features performing sea lions, dolphins, and other creatures, while an investment group headed by Doubleday bought the New York Mets.

The changes that corporations have introduced into their recently acquired publishing companies—beyond putting their accounting men on the scene, providing centralized computer and other services, and, of course, making available large pools of corporate money—have varied considerably. But for the most part the mergers have been followed not only by the introduction of many new management people, more familiar than their predecessors with big-organization procedures, but also by a spread—diffuse and generalized though it may be—within the acquired companies' own staffs of practices normal in the big-corporation world; for example, image-building, marketing, and the setting of production and "performance" quotas. One sign of this sort of adaptation is that, as time goes on, the language of the corporate merchandiser seems ever more a part of the workaday speech of book publishers and editors. Indeed, much of what publishers and editors are doing is becoming ever more closely entangled with what advertising men, television producers and talk-show hosts, and Hollywood producers and packagers are doing.

By way of examining this entanglement, one might consider the role that television talk shows have come to play in publishing. Twenty years ago, the promotion of most trade books was carried out on a relatively genteel and pinchpenny scale, being confined largely to ads taken out under modest advertising budgets in the daily or weekly book-review sections of newspapers, supplemented on occasion by personal appearances of authors at bookstore autographing sessions. The publicity departments of publishing houses usually consisted of one or two people (usually women and therefore underpaid even by the standards prevailing in the publishing business), whose work was usually limited to putting out routine press releases about new books and sending out review copies. But the leisurely attitude of publishers toward publicity began to change when they realized that an appearance by a writer on a television talk show could sometimes have a remarkably stimulating effect on the sales of his or her book. They were given an intimation of television's potential for promoting books by the appearances, beginning in 1959, of Alexander King, a former editor and artist, who, because of serious illness, had become a drug addict for several years. King, a ready and endlessly anecdotal talker, became a favorite guest of Jack Paar on the "Tonight Show," and when a book of his reminiscences called *Mine Enemy Grows Older* was publicized by Paar on the program, the book, which was published by Simon & Schuster, went right onto the *Times* best-seller list. A second book by King, *May This House Be Safe from Tigers,* which Paar also touted to the late-night audience during appearances by its author, sold nearly a hundred and fifty thousand copies in hardcover alone.

In the meantime, a few insiders who were aware of what television publicity could do for books were hard at work. Among them was a former editor at Prentice-Hall named Bernard Geis. At Prentice-Hall in 1957, Geis had put out a book by Art Linkletter called *Kids Say the Darndest Things,* which was a compilation of material from Linkletter's TV show. The book became a top nonfiction title on the *Times* best-seller list and stayed on the list for over a year. "Linkletter told me that the success of the book was primarily due to the fact that he had promoted it on his own show," Geis told me. Linkletter was so enthusiastic about the possibilities that this sort of thing offered to people who, like him, owned, or were the principal figures on, TV shows that—together with Groucho Marx, the star of "You Bet Your Life;" Ralph Edwards, the host of "This Is Your Life;" and the TV producers John Guedel, Mark Goodson, and William Todman—he financed Geis in setting up a book-publishing company, Bernard Geis Associates, that, according to the publisher's scheme, would specialize in the publication of books that would be readily promotable by the hosts or guests of television shows, not excluding the shows being run by the financial backers of Bernard Geis Associates. As could perhaps have been foreseen, among the books that emerged from the innovative house of Geis were *The Secret World of Kids*, by Art Linkletter, and *Harpo Speaks*—both of them handsomely plugged by the authors on various shows.

One of the books that Geis Associates put out was called *Every Night, Josephine!* It was about a poodle and was written by a woman named Jacqueline Susann. *Every Night, Josephine!* sold well, making it onto one nonfiction bestseller list briefly in 1963. In 1966, Miss Susann sent the manuscript of another book to Geis. It was a novel about three girls who separately came to New York in search of romance and success in show business and social life but, in their ambitious climb, took to pill-popping and couldn't get out of the habit. Against the advice of a couple of his editors, who even by the standards of Geis books condemned Miss Susann's new work as "literary trash," Geis published the manuscript. The book was called *Valley of the Dolls*, and though Geis promoted it with an unusual amount of print advertising, by far his main promotional effort consisted in getting Miss Susann on as many television and radio interview shows as possible to talk up her book. In this, he had the full coöperation of Miss Susann, who—under the personal management of her husband, a former Hollywood publicist and television producer named Irving Mansfield—conducted a cross-country campaign to publicize her book on TV and radio shows and also made herself available for innumerable appearances at bookstores, shopping centers, and so on. According to Geis, Miss Susann got on so many TV and radio shows that "someone said then the only thing you could turn on without getting Jacqueline Susann was the water faucet.'' The effect on the sales of *Valley of the Dolls* was remarkable. It sold three hundred and fifty thousand copies in hardcover and stayed on the best-seller list for almost a year and a half, and when the book was issued in paperback—by Bantam Books, in 1967—Miss Susann, aided by a new round of promotional hoopla, with organizational help provided by a young woman named Esther Margolis, who had become Bantam's first publicity director, and a Los Angeles press agent named Jay Allen, set out on yet another relentless cross-country tour of TV and radio talk shows and personal appearances. According to Miss Margolis, who went on to become a senior vice-president of Bantam and later on founded her own publishing company, Newmarket Press, the constant exposure on TV and radio had a huge, direct effect on the popularity of Miss Susann's book and on the enthusiasm of paperback retailers. In paperback, *Valley of the Dolls* sold more than twenty-two million copies.

With such spectacular examples of the potential of television talk shows for boosting the sales of certain kinds of books, a number of publishers began to build up their publicity staffs and their contacts with talk-show production people. This was happening at the time that the number of television talk shows and the size of their audiences were increasing. The relationship that developed between the trade-book publishers and the television people was one of barter. To exist, the talk-show business needs an endless supply of guests, and the publishers found that by getting authors of books on their current lists to appear they could help satisfy that need. The TV people got these guests at no cost to the producers, and the publishers could put their authors on programs at no cost beyond the authors' travelling expenses to and from the TV studios. By the mid-nineteen-seventies, the practice of placing authors on television shows had come to play a fundamental part in the economics of book publishing. Authors of newly published books were routinely sent out on regional or cross-country talk-show tours by the hundred as, in effect, unsalaried representatives of their publishers' sales forces. The authors contributed their working time, received travelling expenses, and waited to see what effect, if any, their being exposed to television audiences would have on the sales of their books. Publishers have found that when authors unfamiliar with the ways of show business are sent out on TV tours, a certain amount of preparation may be advisable, not only concerning the logistics of getting to studios in strange cities but often also concerning how, literally, to put the best face on things.

A "Memo on Media Exposure" given to McGraw-Hill authors by the company's trade-book publicity department offers neophytes to the air some general advice, including the desired comportment of a writer before the cameras, and it also lists some of the hazards that may be encountered. *"Do not underestimate the value of a minor show,"* the memo advises the authors soothingly, just in case one or another of them may feel that the shows listed on the tour schedule don't quite seem to live up to his or her expectations. "Such a program may provide valuable exposure to an audience that would not be reached otherwise." It goes on, "Resolve to be at your best on every show, regardless of your opinion of its format or host." Authors are also urged to suppress their reaction to a discovery they might make just as they go before the cameras: "Do not feel incensed if [the talk-show host] has obviously not read your book. This happens on top-notch shows as well." What would be a lot worse would be to discover that there wasn't a copy of the book itself on the premises. So:

Always bring a copy of your book with you. They may not

have it on hand, it may have been filched—safe is safe. Assume that your interviewer has NOT looked through the book; be prepared to give a quick capsule-summary of its contents. Radio and TV commercials [that interrupt the show periodically] can be put to good use, as during that time you can quietly mention to the host what topics you would like to hit next.

The memo goes on to describe the standard that writers are expected to live up to:

A measure of showmanship is definitely in order. By agreeing to appear before a TV camera or behind a radio mike, you have temporarily assumed the obligations of a show-biz personality. You must radiate self-confidence, charm, charisma. Keep in mind that your normal hand and head gestures will lose all impact when reduced to a TV screen: do not fear to over-gesticulate within reason. . . . Also practice to vary the pitch, tonal qualities and volume of your voice—the purpose is to add strength, punch and interest to your delivery. . . .

For every point you make, have two or three stock examples that *illustrate your statement quickly and memorably.* Be armed with a supply of well thought out, brief personal anecdotes, and pertinent, relevant aphorisms which will sound as if they had just occurred to you and are being ad-libbed on the spur of the moment. . . .

Do not hesitate to mention the title of your book from time to time, and your publisher at least once. . . . Never refer to "my book"—always mention the title, were it only for the benefit of that part of the audience which always tunes in late.

The extent and the effectiveness of the regional or cross-country tours vary widely, of course, from author to author, from publisher to publisher, and from book to book. One author I know who agreed to sally forth on an out-of-town tour of talk shows to publicize a book recalls as one of the less inspiring occasions an interview held in the basement studio of a radio station of depressingly low wattage during which he discovered that the interviewer, who came up with very few questions and seemed preoccupied with some papers in front of him while the author answered what questions there were, was passing the time by going over figures on a work sheet related to his federal income tax. At the other end of the scale, a while after Peter Benchley's book *Jaws*—which Doubleday published in hardcover in 1974, and which has sold more than two hundred thousand copies in that form—was published in paperback by Bantam, in 1976, Benchley hit the TV circuit on a tour organized by the ever-energetic Esther Margolis. The tour came on top of the release of *Jaws* as a movie, and, with the exposure through TV, radio, and the film, sales of the paperback edition jumped from four million to eight million.

Taken as a whole, the effect of TV appearances by authors on the sales of books has made such an impression on book publishers that the art of putting authors on TV has become a sort of mini-industry in itself. The publicity department of every major publishing house is becoming increasingly centered on authors' TV appearances; even the august house of Knopf has a department devoted to everything involving media promotion. Simon Michael Bessie, who is now a senior vice-president of Harper & Row, concedes that television appearances by authors "have become a principal ingredient for the promotion of books." Insuring these appearances, he says, is part of "the struggle in publishing . . . to get attention in a crowded marketplace." This struggle, Bessie says, has shifted to TV partly because of the limited coverage and discussion of books in printed reviews. "The *Times Book Review,* in fifty-two weeks, can review or mention a maximum of perhaps two thousand books, out of about twenty thousand books of general interest that are published each year—only one out of ten," he told me. "Television can be used to call attention to books that don't necessarily get reviewed in print. Television consumes words, people, pictures at an immeasurable rate. It needs subjects, people. Book publishers can provide them. The two interests coincide.'' Donna Schrader, the publicity director of Dial Press, describing the advantages to talk-show producers of having authors on their programs, says, ''It's *fodder* for their shows.'' From the publishers' point of view, arranging for authors' tours is a far cheaper way than print advertising of reaching large audiences. Illustrating this point, Jane Becker Friedman, the director of promotion for Knopf, says, ''A full-page ad for a book in the *Times Book Review* costs seventy-five hundred dollars. For seventy-five hundred dollars, we can send an author on a major talk-show tour of ten cities, and the total TV audience reached might be reckoned in the tens of millions rather than in the millions reached through a *Times* ad.'' Donna Schrader on the same subject: ''If you counted up what we get in author appearances on TV and radio practically for free, and added up all these words at advertising prices—wow! What an advertising budget we'd have!''

The extent of the national author-supply business, a sort of chandlery of the air, is indicated by the long lists of forthcoming tours by authors which are issued in publishing newsletters and other publications. *Publishers Weekly* regularly devoted a section to a listing of forthcoming authors' tours until recently, when, it seems, the list got so unwieldy that the editors decided to deal with only the more important tours, as part of another section. On the main editorial floor of the Fifth Avenue headquarters of Bantam Books, a passing glimpse of that part of Bantam's promotion department which is devoted to authors' tours gives an impression of feverish activity—telephones go like mad as contacts are made with authors, talk-show production people, airline offices, hotels, and so on, and the results of all these negotiations are condensed in the form of tour schedules listed on a big Plexiglas board. The calculations concerning the potential sales effectiveness of placing an author on one talk show rather than another in the same city have become so fine that the publicity directors at some major publishing houses keep on hand, among other reference works, television-industry tabulations of both the size and the composition of audiences reached by competing talk shows.

Thus, in sending an author to Chicago to make a television appearance, the promotion director of a publishing house might ponder the advantages of getting him or her on "AM Chicago," which goes on between nine and nine-thirty, rather than the Lee Phillip show, "Noonbreak," or the "NewsCenter 5" show, also at noon. One of these promotion people outlined for me the calculations to be made: "All right, 'AM Chicago' has a three rating, with an audience of ninety thousand adults, of whom seventy thousand are women and twenty thousand are men. The Lee Phillip show has a five rating and a hundred and sixty thousand viewers, of whom a hundred and thirty-four thousand are women and twenty-six thousand are men. The 'NewsCenter 5' show has a six rating and a total audience of two hundred and ten thousand, with a hundred and thirty-six thousand women and seventy-four thousand men. Suppose you decide to try getting the author on one of the noon shows, which have higher ratings than 'AM Chicago.' 'NewsCenter 5' has a six rating versus a five for Lee Phillip. But if your author has a book that you figure is going to appeal mainly to women, the numbers are actually about the same for the two shows. Who is it that you're after? If the author has a book that deals with, say, politics, which is more likely to appeal to men, 'NewsCenter 5' is definitely the show to shoot for, since it gives you an audience that contains fifty thousand more men than the Lee Phillip show." Then, there are further intricacies, usually beyond the technical understanding of the author being dispatched around the circuit but of considerable concern to the publisher's publicity people. The promotion director remarked, "Lee Phillip will not take an author who has already appeared on 'AM Chicago' during his tour. But if 'AM Chicago' is out of the picture and Lee Phillip does agree to take the author, you know that you aren't going to stand a chance with Jorie Lueloff, who interviews authors on WMAQ—an NBC affiliate—but who won't take one who has just appeared with Lee Phillip.''

Of course, there are other reasons that an author may not get the opportunity to appear on one of these shows to discuss his or her book. The author may be cursed with an inappropriately shy or diffident manner, or be too slow of speech, or talk with a cracked voice, or have a squint or some little facial tic—or may in general fail to "radiate self-confidence, charm, charisma.'' In such unfortunate cases, the head of promotion at the author's publishing house can simply exercise the publisher's prerogative of not putting the author on tour at all, on the principle that his appearance might actually dissuade TV audiences from going out and buying the book. Publishers are particularly concerned about putting authors who have a less than persuasive manner on such big network or syndicated shows as "Today,'' "Tonight,'' "Tomorrow,'' "Good Morning, America,'' "Merv Griffin,'' "Dick Cavett,'' and "Donahue.'' When such matters are being considered, the interests of author and publisher are not necessarily given the same weight. Many of the authors who go on "Today'' don't just go on cold. By way of preparation for such a big-time appearance, the publisher may send an author off on the talk-show equivalent of a theatrical out-of-town tryout, in which he will make appearances on lesser talk shows, which do not compete with it. (They must certainly not compete. Is the "Today'' show likely to invite an author who has just been saying his piece on its hated competitor "Good Morning, America''?) The promotion director at one major hardcover house said to me, "We believe that the 'Today' show or

'Donahue' should not be the first appearance for an author. We send him out to other shows, and he comes back better prepared and more confident on camera. We try to talk to him about what these appearances entail. We impress on him the need for *energy* on TV—if he doesn't display it, we won't sell the book and the show will lose the audience. And we have our own relations with the producer of the show to consider. It might be a one-shot, all-or-nothing book for the author, and he might not even think of being on the show again, but I have to go back to Donahue.''

Jay Allen, the Los Angeles press agent whose efforts contributed to getting the pioneering Jacqueline Susann on so many television and radio shows, and who, acting under contract to publishers, has managed over the years to get some four hundred and fifty authors on TV and radio interview shows, said to me, speaking of some authors yet unseasoned by constant proximity to microphones and TV cameras, ''They spend their lives over a typewriter, and think of what goes on paper, so it's not at all unusual for us to have a little training course with them, in which I take on the role of interviewer. So many of these authors don't know the value of an anecdote, and if you're going to hold an audience on a talk show, it's with anecdotes. In these practice sessions, I'll correct their way of answering questions. I'll say, 'No, no—don't answer that way, think of an anecdote!' ''

Allen let me know that he was a strong advocate of the advantages of getting authors of his client publishers on radio as well as on TV, especially on the West Coast, because the heavy driving done there means that a large audience is constantly exposed to programs on car radios. ''In L.A., if we're trying to reach a more literate audience, I go to Michael Jackson. On his radio show, he has an hour with each author, and he opens his lines for call-ins for the last twenty-five minutes, drawing on your academic group, and you don't get your ding-a-ling fringe that you hear on so many call-in shows.''

Paul Friedman, a former producer of the "Today" show, seemed bemused, when I talked to him, by the way publishers put their authors on the television tryout circuit. "I mean, they take their authors around, run these people ragged," he remarked some time ago. "The publishers make their decisions on whom they're going to push and on what shows, then they push them. And you become part of the whole system. I assume the publishers are sitting over there in their offices and thinking, How are the television people going to fill up their programs without having authors on? They figure that what we've got in author appearances is the cheapest possible way of filling air time—that it costs us nothing to bring an author in on the show. And to a certain extent the publishers are right. It doesn't cost me a film crew and all those travelling expenses to interview an author—it *is* cheaper for us, having one brought into the studio. It certainly costs the *publisher* nothing, or next to nothing, to put an author on a show. Publishers try for all they can get. A number of them come to us and say, 'Will you take out an ad together with us'— about an author's forthcoming appearance—'with *the television show* paying for the ad?' They want every ounce of blood!'' In reaction to this sort of thing, the "Today" people seem to have become more selective in the last couple of years about the authors they put on as guests, but the appearance of an author on "Today" is considered one of the biggest promotional prizes around for any publisher. Friedman himself said, "A Book-of-the-Month selection is more important for a publisher than a 'Today' appearance by the author, but the 'Today' appearance is the second most important thing.''

One of the curious aspects of the promotion of books by authors' appearances on television shows is the kind of book that tends to get pushed. Of course, the range of books discussed and plugged on the air in interviews with their authors is slightly constricted by the general refusal of certain authors, such as Saul Bellow, John Hersey, Philip Roth, Bernard Malamud, and Anne Tyler, to engage in this sort of promotion; still, other distinguished writers, such as Norman Mailer, Joseph Heller, and Isaac Bashevis Singer, have appeared on the air to discuss their work. But, beyond these considerations, the books discussed on talk shows are usually nonfiction works, because talk-show hosts find it difficult to discuss works of fiction on the air. For one thing, an interviewer more or less has to have actually *read* a work of fiction fairly carefully just to know the plot, and certainly to absorb the psychic complexities that may be conveyed by the author on the printed page. But with nonfiction works a talk-show host can be filled in by his assistants and scriptwriters, and need not have done much more than skim through the book himself to determine its general subject matter—a situation that usually leads to talk about the author's involvement with the subject.

Publishers try to get around the anti-fiction obstacle by offering the producers fiction writers who can discuss the factual situations underlying their subject matter. This technique owes much to the trailblazing efforts of Jacqueline Susann, whose inspiration it was to go before the talk-show cameras and discuss not the meanderings of plot in *Valley of the Dolls* but such things as the scandal of pill-popping by rich and famous women in general. ''As a matter of fact, Jackie didn't so much *discuss* as *deny* on those talk shows,'' Bernard Geis remarked to me. ''She would *deny* that the characters were based on well-known real people. She would *deny* that one character was really modelled on Judy Garland. She would *deny* that it was really Ethel Merman she was portraying in the book.'' Miss Susann denied her way across the country, and her book sales soared triumphantly. The principle has lived on and flourished in TV. The roman à clef continues to be a successful vehicle for publishers eager to insure attention on the air to writers of fiction, and the promotion people at publishing houses frequently offer talk-show producers real-life topics into which the fictional works of one or another of their authors might be fitted. "You send them a good pitch letter, and some suggested questions, and you talk to the author and go over the whole thing with him," one promotion director said a while ago. Nevertheless, the major efforts that publishers make to get authors on TV are in connection with writers of nonfiction works. Norman Mailer might go on TV to discuss *The Executioner's Song,* his novelistic treatment of the life of the murderer Gary Gilmore, or Henry Kissinger might have gone on to discuss his memoirs, but a lot of the writers who go on are people like Dr. Wayne Dyer, who wrote *Your Erroneous Zones,* a book of psychological self-help published by T. Y. Crowell in 1976. *"Your Erroneous Zones* was *absolutely made* on television," a Crowell publicity woman told me. On the strength of a big coast-to-coast TV tour by the author, the book sold more than eight hundred thousand copies in hardcover, and nearly five million copies have been printed in paperback.

Though the direct influence of talk shows on the sale of books may apply chiefly to books on what the promotion director of one hardcover publishing house refers to as "subjects natural to the talk-show market—anything to do with marriage, divorce, mental and physical self-improvement," the practice of bartering television time for free appearances by authors has also had a broad general effect on the publishing business. For one thing, sending authors on talk-show tours has become such an integral part of the trade-book economy that it is difficult to conceive of any publisher's being able to discontinue the practice, even if he wanted to, without detriment to his company's competitive standing; and this conviction may attract the publishing houses to those authors who seem capable of becoming public "personalities." In fact, in the whole process of putting a manuscript into book form and getting it to readers, the consideration of the author as a public personality is coming to be less and less a matter of pure chance. And estimates of an author's potential as a public personality, rather than just as a writer, tend to be made earlier and earlier in the game. Still, apart from those few publishers who, like Bernard Geis in his *Valley of the Dolls* phase, may have centered their publishing operations almost exclusively on highly promotable authors, it is unlikely that any manuscript would be turned down because the author told his prospective publisher that he had no intention of going on TV or radio to plug the work. But there is little doubt that when an author expresses enthusiasm at the prospect of doing his promotional bit for his publisher—and when the promotion people at the publishing house feel that he might come off well on the tube—his work can be published in an encouraging atmosphere. With no such publicity boost in sight, sales of a book have to rely primarily on favorable newspaper and magazine reviews. Formerly, publishers also tended to apply a sliding-scale allocation (related to the size of the initial printing and the retail price of the book) of paid print advertising, but nowadays a book that isn't boosted on television may get no advertising appropriation at all. In addition, the money put into advertising often depends on how quotable the reviews are. Of course, for most authors and their publishers exposure on television talk shows may not make much difference in the size of the book sales, but it certainly makes enough difference in enough instances so that publishers are paying increasing attention to what television exposure can accomplish. One effect is that, as Simon Michael Bessie remarked, "it's the author as a personality rather than the book as a book" that tends to get put forward on television and to be considered by the viewing public. Another consequence arises out of the fact that television not only serves in itself as a powerful direct propagator of popular images but also makes a very responsive connection with other mass media, which it continually feeds on and sucks material out of. As commercial television has inculcated in mass audiences the concept of the personality-author, it has at the same time helped to provide publishers with tempting visions of a new *scale* on which books—of a certain kind, at least—might be promoted and sold, through the use of multimedia techniques and the blockbuster approach.

CHAPTER 3

Chain-Store Systems

ONE OF THE MOST important trends—be-
sides mergers—to affect the publishing industry in the last
twenty years has been the remarkable growth of big bookstore chains—a development that has been paralleled by a
decline in the prosperity, and even the numbers, of independent booksellers. This is not to imply that (except in
unusual circumstances) the spread of the big book chains
has been the direct cause of the decline of independent
booksellers, in the way that big grocery chains once caused
the demise of small local grocery stores—by undercutting
their prices until the local merchants gave up the unequal
struggle, whereupon the chain groceries put their prices up.
The independent booksellers' difficulties are not ordinarily
a matter of chains' moving into the independents' territory
and doing them in by selling books at cut-rate prices. By
and large, the big national chains—and this is certainly true
of the two largest, B. Dalton Booksellers and Waldenbooks—do not sell current books at cut-rate prices, nor do
they appear to have made a general policy of moving in on
the physical territory of independent bookstores. Although
in recent times some of them have opened branches in
downtown areas of some large cities, thereby possibly con-

tributing to the difficulties of existing independent book-sellers in these areas, on the whole the chains have tended to occupy new territories, where few, if any, bookstores existed before—primarily in suburban shopping malls and other high-traffic areas within easy walking distance of parking lots. They have thrived on a policy of high-volume sales, quick turnover of stock, highly computerized systems of accounting and inventory control, and large-scale purchasing.

Without such advantages, and under the stress of inflationary pressures, independent booksellers have had an increasingly difficult time over the past decade. One of their problems has been the soaring postal rates for hardcover books. Independent bookstores—and chain bookstores as well—receive bulk shipments of hardcover books from two main sources: directly from the publisher, or through national book-distribution organizations. While most big shipments arrive by truck, a considerable number of books reach retail outlets by parcel post. Unlike chain bookstores, independent bookstores have traditionally devoted themselves to serving the individual needs and reading preferences of loyal customers, by obtaining, by special order, books not in stock. Usually, these books are sent from the publishers directly to the bookseller by mail, the postage being paid by the bookseller. In the past, obtaining books for customers by special order often accounted for as much as twenty per cent of the business, and when postal rates were still moderate the bookseller was able to absorb the postal costs and make a reasonable profit on special orders. But in the last decade the rates have risen so rapidly that a typical hardcover book, weighing two pounds, which in 1970 might have cost the bookseller eighteen cents in postage, cost him eighty-one cents in 1980. That represented an increase of three hundred and fifty per cent—and over the same period the average retail price of a hardcover trade book rose at about a quarter that rate.

Further, independent booksellers complain that the major trade publishers are imposing on them a maximum discount rate of forty per cent of a book's list price while offering the big chains discounts of between forty-two and forty-six per cent. While most independent booksellers understand the equity of publishers' allowing the chains some extra discount for large purchases, they say that for many individual store owners those percentage points of difference in their discount rate mean the difference between profit and loss. They charge that the discount practices amount to discriminatory treatment, and that this treatment contributes to a serious reduction of competition in the bookselling industry.

Whatever the merits of these claims, there is no doubt that independent booksellers are playing a rapidly diminishing role in publishing. In 1958, sixty-five per cent of the trade books sold in this country were from the output of the fifty largest trade-book publishers. By 1977, sixty per cent of the trade books sold were supplied by the *ten* largest trade publishers. A parallel concentration has been evident in the bookselling business. In 1972, the four largest bookstore chains accounted for about eleven and a half per cent of all trade-book sales in the country, but by the end of 1979 just the two largest chains accounted for something like a third of all trade-book and mass-market-paperback sales, and, according to current projections, by 1983 those two chains may account for around half of such sales. By contrast, one-store independent booksellers, who in 1958 were selling seventy-two per cent of the trade books bought in this country, in 1980 accounted for something less than forty per cent of the total number of these sales.

Such statistics so disturbed Maxwell J. Lillienstein, the general counsel for the American Booksellers Association—

a national trade association with five thousand three hundred members, drawn from both the independents and the chains—that in 1979 he temporarily stepped out of his role as A.B.A. counsel and, writing on his own behalf, in an article printed in the A.B.A.'s trade publication *American Bookseller,* accused "the behemoths of the book-publishing industry" of "pushing most independent booksellers to the brink of financial disaster" by discriminatory discounting and other inequitable trade practices, which he condemned as "unconscionable, if not unlawful." And Lillienstein told me that a 1977 study commissioned by the A.B.A. showed that most independent booksellers either were existing on a marginal basis or were actually operating at a loss; that since then the plight of many of them had become "much worse;" and that if the operators of these bookstores were not afforded some relief from prevailing trade-discount practices and other, comparably burdensome practices, before long we would see "a general demise of the independent booksellers."

The style of the chain bookstore represents a sharp break from that of the traditional independent bookstore, with its pleasant clutter, its subdued aura, its slow-to-budge browsers, and its attentive proprietor. The chain bookstores are brightly lighted, with bold-colored displays, and often with racks laid out in irregular angled patterns that oblige the customer to pass a carefully calculated maximum shelf area of books in moving from one part of the store to another; the design of these stores aims at inducing the customer to make multiple purchases. The merchandising style of the chain stores is well suited to that of the suburban shopping centers and shopping malls in which they are so often situated. As an institution, the suburban shopping center is built around the supermarket, the giant parking lot, and the replacement of traditional behind-the-counter salesmanship by a system of pre-selling customers on the virtues of particular products through television commercials, through point-of-purchase displays, through prominent displays of loss-leader products, and through the use of every other conceivable device to hasten the impulse buying of brand-name goods.

It is hard to think of two institutions in contemporary American life more perfectly attuned than commercial television and the supermarket system. And in the suburban shopping center the chain bookstore has provided an almost literal extension of supermarket shopping. A woman who walks into one of these bookstores may just have come from the supermarket across the way, where, in addition to her other purchases, she may have picked up at the checkout counter a copy of *People* magazine, a publication that, among other things, regularly chronicles the lives of big-time popular authors. She may also have seen the same authors hustling their books on the "Today" show, "Donahue," the "Tonight Show," "The Merv Griffin Show," and so on. When she looks in at the bookstore after her supermarket shopping, she sees all the books she has been hearing about. The atmosphere inside the bookstore is so much like that of the supermarket—bright lighting, big displays of popular items, stretches of shelf space, and merchandising islands conveniently laid out—that she can continue her impulse buying with hardly a change of pace. The managers of these stores may know about books, but they usually aren't particularly visible, and as likely as not the few assistants on hand are young people occupied with the job of filling shelves, who seldom discuss books with customers. In my experience, the atmosphere in some of these stores is far from attractive, but in some—including the bigger stores of the B. Dalton chain—it is by no means uninviting. The very scarcity of visible human help seems to be part of the design of a B. Dalton store, not merely to save on labor costs but also to make the shopping-center customer comfortable. "We try for a bright-colored, cartoony feeling in our stores," a B. Dalton advertising and promotion executive told me some time ago. "When the customers walk in, they shouldn't feel they have to whisper, the way they might in the old-style bookstore. We use the phrase 'We take the awesomeness out of the book-buying experience.' Many people tend to feel intimidated when they go into a bookstore. You have no sense of intimidation in our stores."

The B. Dalton operation arose as a result of the expansion of the Dayton Hudson Corporation, a company formed by the merger of two big department stores—one in Minneapolis and one in Detroit. The first B. Dalton bookstore was opened in a suburban Dayton shopping mall in 1966; in 1969—by which time two other B. Dalton stores had been opened in other shopping malls—the Dayton Hudson Corporation bought the well-known Pickwick Bookshop, in Hollywood, and other Pickwick outlets; and three years later the company merged the two operations under the name B. Dalton Booksellers. By the end of 1979, there were more than four hundred and fifty B. Dalton stores, and the company expects to have eight hundred in operation across the country by 1983. The advertising executive gave this description of a typical B. Dalton store: "We look for multiple purchases all the time. We work the impulse areas very hard. The checkout area is especially conducive to impulse buying. We use table displays and dump bins"— freestanding prefabricated display racks—"for best-sellers, and you have to walk by different displays of the same books two or three times when you go through the store." Interestingly, the average number of book titles in a B. Dalton store is about twenty-five thousand (compared with perhaps ten thousand titles in an average independent bookstore in a medium-sized city), and the Dalton people insist that their basic business revolves not simply around best-sellers but around "the less-than-best-sellers." Just the same, those impulse areas are indeed worked very hard.

One striking aspect of the big national chains is the relationship that has developed between them and the publishing industry. Unlike traditional independent booksellers, whose reaction to whatever they have been supplied with is usually rather slow, and is reflected mainly in the bare sales figures eventually compiled for particular books, the big chains have taken an active role in signalling to publishers what is likely to sell in their stores and what isn't. In fact, the B. Dalton organization, in particular, seems to represent a certain initiating force in the big-book business as well as an effective selling force. What the B. Dalton people indicate that they think about a book at the bound-proof stage, prior to publication, or even earlier than that, can have a considerable effect on its fortunes after publication, and their opinions are eagerly sought after within the publishing business. A pale-green printed memorandum called the *B. Dalton Merchandise Bulletin,* which is prepared by Kay Sexton, a B. Dalton vice-president, and sent out weekly to all B. Dalton stores, and also to most publishers, is closely studied at trade-publishing houses, hardcover or paperback, and has become one of the most influential publications in the entire book-publishing business. Along with brief reviews of recommended current books, the *Merchandise Bulletin* gives up-to-date lists of "Hot-List Titles" and of "B. Dalton Bestsellers" in hardcover form and in both mass-market- and trade-paperback form—lists that are compiled with remarkable speed and accuracy, because they are based on data taken from computers that are directly connected to cash registers in all B. Dalton stores and tell precisely how many copies of all books on sale have been bought by the chain's customers. The *Merchandise Bulletin* also contains a three- or four-page section entitled "Promotion/Publicity," which lists the city-by-city schedules of forthcoming national and regional TV and radio talk-show tours by authors of popular books, so that appropriate displays and special sales of their books can be arranged to coincide with this public exposure. Publishers' promotion departments regularly alert the chain-store people well ahead of time—usually long before publication date—to the touring plans laid out for authors, and also fill them in in other ways on the promise of certain books for hitting the big time. "We're always being told how great the author is, and how the author is *promotable*," a Dalton executive remarked to me some time ago.

So sought after by publishers is the judgment of the big chains concerning the successful presentation of books that some of them will take to the headquarters of a bookstore chain sample copies of certain yet-to-be-published books which have been bound with different cover designs and illustrations. The chain then coöperates with the publisher in setting up panels of customers in several of its retail stores to give their reaction, and thus helps to determine such matters as whether a book with one cover design "makes a difference in customer pickup"—as one chain-bookstore executive has put it—relative to the same book with another design. What the future holds for this sort of thing is unknown, but informal communication between publishers and the chains has grown to the extent that I have heard it said that some major hardcover publishers just will not go ahead with the publication of a certain book until they have obtained what they consider an encouraging reaction from the big bookstore chains about its chances for selling well. One man who is very knowledgeable about the business recently said to me, "I've been told by people at the mass-market-paperback houses that their decision to promote a book in a big way or not is based on the extent to which the chains indicate they'll be prepared to carry the book." The B. Dalton people themselves look upon their relationships with publishers as mutually beneficial—entirely in the interests of their being able to sell, in the words of a B. Dalton executive, "better books better, and faster, and to the most people."

No doubt the chains have been very successful in bringing many books to many people. And they have done so by bringing to a poorly organized business the efficiency of modern merchandising and the point-of-sale techniques that are part of the supermarket age. One chain-bookstore executive told me, "We're not going to make George Gissing fans out of people—we're mass-merchandising the product." The computers attached to the cash registers in B. Dalton stores enable the chain to run an elaborate and instantly reactive stock-control system, and also enable the people who are running the chains to know precisely and immediately how well particular books—and, beyond that, what particular *kinds* of books—are selling. By the same token, computer data may be used to tell them, with almost equal speed, and down to the last calculable foot of shelf space, which books are not measuring up to the appropriate standards of what supermarket merchandisers refer to as "item velocity." The titles that don't measure up aren't reordered. And copies still on hand may be rather quickly shipped back to the publishers. An executive of one bookstore chain explained to me, "You can't afford to keep these books around forever. We keep back stock, yes, but very few books in our stores become basic back-stock items." This is not to overlook the fact that the man who runs an independent store has his own routine of thinning out and disposing of stock that isn't selling well; but without computerized inventory-control systems the winnowing-out process is slower, more laborious, more merely human, and is tempered by the individual judgment of the bookstore owner concerning the intrinsic merit of particular books and by his intimate knowledge of the preferences of particular customers who may yet come by. In general, his method of winnowing allows many books that sell only modestly a comparatively long lease on life, whereas their chances for survival in a chain store would be precarious. Inventory and sales printouts can occasionally reveal an unexpected customer interest in a "small" book, resulting in its further promotion within the stores, but, for the most part, in the computerized chain-store system books that don't attain the requisite velocity tend to get washed out to sea in the undertow from the incessant incoming waves of new bestsellers, accompanied as they are by the churning displays of publicity and media promotion. And it is to such dynamics of high-visibility, high-velocity, supermarket-style merchandising that the publishing industry appears to be accommodating itself more and more.

CHAPTER 4

An Escalation of Risk

THE FACT that by 1977 the ten largest publishing companies were accounting for sixty per cent of all trade-book sales in this country is matched, as an indicator of concentration in the book business, by the fact that in the same year the eight largest mass-market-paperback houses (all of them conglomerate-owned) were accounting for eighty-four per cent of all mass-market-paperback sales. The distribution system for paperbacks also displays elements of concentration. Paperback books are distributed on the wholesale level in three principal ways. The first is through a system of national distribution companies, of which there are nine major ones. Each of these distribution companies represents one or more paperback houses on a more or less exclusive basis, and most are owned by the conglomerate or the big communications company that also owns the paperback house or houses involved. These national distributors deliver books to about five hundred regional or local independent distributors, known in the trade as I.D.s. In turn, the independent distributors sell the paperbacks to retailers, to whom they deliver the books by truck. Besides dealing in mass-market paperbacks, some of these I.D.s may handle trade paperbacks that are issued by the publishing houses the national distributors represent, and some of them may also handle books put out by other paperback publishers, but with the important provision that these will not be in categories thought to compete with those of their big suppliers.

Mass-market books put out by the big paperback houses—there are just nine of these—or by the several dozen lesser ones may also reach retailers through national or regional jobbers. But by and large, as things stand, no outside publisher can expect to enter the mass-market-paperback business on a truly competitive basis without setting up his own national distribution system and obtaining the effective coöperation of the established independent distributors and national jobbers. The independent distributors operate as exclusive franchisers within their particular territories. Their basic business is the distribution of newspapers and magazines to retailers. This business has a rough-and-tumble history that extends back to the newspaper-delivery wars in the nineteen-twenties, with their shotgun-and-blackjack practices. But nowadays—as far as the distribution of mass-market paperbacks is concerned, at least—there seems to be no competitive raiding, even of a peaceful kind, of the territories covered by independent distributors. For all this, the degree of direct control exercised by the independents over just what books they handle seems to be relatively limited.

Magazines and mass-market paperbacks share more than a system of distribution; the independent distributors actually treat mass-market paperbacks after the fashion of magazines—that is, as high-turnover merchandise, having a fleeting shelf life in retail outlets. Like magazines, newly issued mass-market paperbacks are delivered by the I.D.s to retailers in waves. Like magazines, the paperbacks are regarded as returnable merchandise. Such paperbacks are being put on the market at the rate of about two hundred titles a month, and the competition among their publishers to acquire the greatest proportion of the available shelf space in retail outlets has become intense. While independent distributors may theoretically have the final say about which particular books they will handle, it seems that in practice, instead of choosing which titles they are going to distribute to retailers, they allot to each of their publishers a monthly budget, into which the publishers then fit their own array of titles and the number of each title to be supplied. The amount of the budget and other aspects of these arrangements are subject to all sorts of bargaining between publishers and independent distributors, and also to what are, in effect, tie-in sales arrangements. And what such sales are tied to is the big, highly promoted, best-selling book—the blockbuster—because it is by having such "hot" titles at the head of his current list of publications that a mass-market-paperback publisher, through his dickerings with his independent distributors, can maneuver his way into obtaining increased budgetary allocations for his whole line of books, and thus advance his cause in the fight for supremacy in shelf space in the vast, scattered battlefield of drugstores, airport shops, supermarkets, railroad-station newsstands, country stores, and vacation-resort gift shops as well as retail bookstores. A movie producer recently remarked of such sales arrangements with distributors and retailers, "If we tried that in *our* business, the government would call it block booking, which, of course, is illegal."

The reverberations of this struggle for rack space extend to almost every part of the book-publishing industry. The shift of power within the industry from hardcover to paperback publishing and the emphasis on blockbusters as the paperback publishers' main tool for forging themselves a prominent position in the retail stores keep the prices paid for the rights to potential blockbusters escalating rapidly. Inevitably, this escalation has had its effect on the normal editorial structure of the hardcover publishing houses: they are now pouring large amounts of conglomerate money into the big-book sweepstakes in the hope of winning huge prizes from the sale of paperback rights to the most popular books. As this process continues, the emphasis in the hardcover end of the business seems to be relentlessly shifting from simply publishing hardcover books to the business of selling subsidiary rights to those books. Just as big conglomerate money is what enables the hardcover houses to pay out big advances for the potential blockbusters that they hope will allow them to hit the paperback-rights bonanzas, big conglomerate money is what enables the paperback houses to pay out the huge advances for reprint rights to the big-book leaders that will open up rack space for their paperback lines in the retail stores. For all concerned, remaining in the competitive race means risk progressively piled on risk, and pressure on pressure.

Large as the rewards of landing a series of blockbusters on the racks may be, paperback publishers have been expressing increasing concern over the chancy nature of the game, especially in an inflationary situation where the price of a mass-market paperback has risen from less than a dollar to two or three dollars in only a few years. "We are dealing with a very crowded, competitive marketplace," Howard Kaminsky, the president and publisher of Warner Books, which has the reputation of being among the more aggressive mass-market-paperback publishers, remarked to me. "It's like being in every race at a publishing Aqueduct. All the major firms come out with their entries within a two-week or three-week period each month. I'm going in with my big guns—one! two! three!—down the line against Pocket, Bantam, Avon, Ballantine, and the rest. We have limited outlets and very short selling times on the racks. We have learned enough from each other and from our own creative juices to use maximum effort in promoting and packaging our books.'' But Kaminsky went on to say, of the escalation of the prices commonly being demanded by hardcover houses and paid by mass-market-paperback houses for big books, and of the actual risks inherent in the paperback marketplace, that he had begun to wonder whether the economics of publishing could fundamentally support the big-book price structure imposed on it by the competitive pressures. ''At the best, the bonanza in mass-market publishing when you hit it does not yield the kind of profits that the movie business or the record business does,'' he said. Oscar Dystel, an old hand in the mass-market-paperback business—having retired as board chairman of Bantam Books, he is now a special consultant to the company—ruefully observed to me about the battle to obtain reprint rights to blockbusters, ''The competition for these books has become incredible. The bidding for rights has become frantic. Those companies with the capital resources are going out and paying these outlandish prices for titles in order to maintain their market share.''

In reaction to the escalation of prices for reprint rights to big sellers, some paperback publishers have been seeking out manuscripts for prices that they consider manageable and publishing them as mass-market originals rather than as reprints. To an increasing degree, they are thinking of themselves as publishers in their own right rather than as mere reprinters, and they speak encouragingly of augmenting their own editorial staffs with experienced manuscript editors. In 1979, for example, New American Library acquired and published *Phoenix,* a thriller by Amos Aricha and Eli Landau. In doing so, it put about a hundred thousand dollars into advertising the book—considerably more than it had paid for the book in the first place. *Phoenix* sold more than a million copies, in paperback. In 1980, Bantam Books issued, as an original work, a new novel by Tom Robbins, the author of *Even Cowgirls Get the Blues.* The new book, which is called *Still Life with Woodpecker,* came out simultaneously in trade paperback and in hardcover, and these editions were followed by a mass-market-paperback edition. Also in 1980, Warner Books published a new work by Richard Nixon, *The Real War,* in hardcover, and used the hardcover distribution facilities of Random House to get it into bookstores across the country. In the spring of 1981, Warner reprinted the book as a mass-market paperback. But none of these developments appear to have slowed down the rise in the huge sums that the mass-market-paperback houses are paying for reprint rights to big books. The bidding and the money just keep going up.

CHAPTER **5**

Agents

Not the least of the reasons for the great increase in the amount of money being paid out for paper-back-reprint rights to popular books is the role that has been played by authors' agents over the last twenty years. There are all sorts of authors' agents, of course, and they have their individual working styles. Some of the agents are extremely efficient, and some are little more than mail drops for manuscripts. Some of them represent their authors well in most respects but may be sufficiently reluctant to disturb their continuing relationships with publishers, with whom they must deal year in and year out, that they are hesitant about doing battle for particular clients over particular issues—such issues as the personal-liability clauses in standard publishing contracts, which commonly require authors to be financially liable for all the costs involved in and damages arising out of libel lawsuits brought against the publisher in connection with an author's work. Many agents represent with equal vigor and skill commercially successful authors and authors who may have talent but haven't achieved any particular success. Some represent their commercially successful authors vigorously and give little time or attention to the others. And some represent only very commercial authors and concentrate almost exclusively on making big deals. The power and influence of this last kind of agent have increased very noticeably in the era of the blockbuster. "Book publishing has become an agent-dominated business," Howard Kaminsky, of Warner Books, told me in discussing the volatile economics of the subsidiary-rights field. Some of the more active of these agents are also lawyers, whose experience both in adversary negotiations and in contract law has made for a new force in the business. This new force is being used to put together blockbuster deals involving a kind of multi-conglomerate interplay of hardcover and mass-market-paperback publishing with television and movie production—an interplay calculated and programmed for maximum effect and employing all available devices of promotion and mass merchandising.

Of the lawyer-agents who have made their mark in the book business in recent years, the one probably most in the public eye is Morton L. Janklow, of the law firm of Janklow, Traum & Klebanoff, who also heads the literary agency Morton L. Janklow Associates. As a lawyer, Janklow is engaged in no litigation; he uses his legal experience to advance the interests of his agency's clients in negotiating contracts between them and publishers, producers, and so on. Among the authors of best-selling novels whom Janklow represents are Sidney Sheldon, who wrote *Bloodline* and *Rage of Angels,* and Judith Krantz, who wrote *Scruples* and *Princess Daisy.* Janklow is a fairly tall man of spare build, with an intense manner and a habit of rapid speech, and in various interviews I had with him at his New York headquarters I found him not at all backward in expressing his views about the current state of the book-publishing business and the direction in which he thinks it should go.

Janklow believes that publishing has, as he puts it, "some wonderful things about it, such as the unique writer-editor relationships that have developed," but that, "with all the charm of the nineteenth century" which the profession has attempted to retain, something has to be done to deal squarely with many of its antiquated practices and to cope with the realities behind the myth of publishing as a genteel profession. "There are a lot of attitudes and techniques being held on to in this business that are not very relevant anymore," Janklow said to me. "We live in a world that is market-oriented. A new element has crept into publishing with the appearance on the scene of people like me—people who are lawyers by training and negotiators by instinct, and who have come into the picture as advocates. And we have started to change some of the financial perspectives of the business, taking into account the various forces at work, such as the influence of television, and considering how these forces affect the exploitive possibilities of a literary work, both in terms of buying the rights to the work and in terms of marketing the work. For good or ill, the old style of editor and publisher is slowly passing from the scene. Now there's a much more energetic, more driving—and, I must say, more profit-oriented—publisher arising."

Janklow said that while some book publishers might feel that they had an obligation to publish fine writing, "the problem is that it takes the important commercial books to fund such publications." All authors are entitled to decent treatment by publishers, he said, and certainly the authors of commercial books ought to be paid in accordance with present-day economic realities. "I think the author is the pivotal person, the star," Janklow said. "Yet I came into the business as an agent and saw that so many writers were being treated like children by publishers. Nobody told them anything. Nobody tried to define for them the publishers' objectives in putting out their work. Here you might have somebody who worked for years writing his book, and it's as though what he produced after all that labor were a baby sent out for adoption—when he handed the manuscript over, he had no more say about it. He might or might not get royalty statements on time and they might or might not be accurate. We're here to be the author's advocate and adviser, and to change that."

As far as Janklow is concerned, the conglomerates have brought many valuable things to publishing. "They have made money available in a serious way, so that people in the business can compete for and pay more for valuable commercial works," he said. "And the conglomerates introduced concepts that go with good corporate planning—budgeting, profit projections and estimates—and they've superimposed these on the old way of doing things in publishing and placed publishers in a commercial atmosphere. Which I don't think is necessarily a harmful thing. Trade-book publishing is, after all, a business that people went into for profit, even in former times. Also, the conglomerates have encouraged decent compensation for good people, and that used to be rare in the business. I know some book editors who are making the kind of money now that was unheard of in publishing even five years ago—people like Michael Korda, the editor-in-chief of Simon & Schuster, who gets paid, and paid very well, for delivering success."

The notion that such a new commercial spirit might be found inappropriate to the customary ethical and business standards of publishers and editors seemed not to perturb Janklow. "It's interesting to think how, because of the way it has evolved, book publishing is so widely regarded as a business of great intellectual achievement—one of the last great gentlemanly businesses in the world," he said. "I've been at the bar for twenty-seven years. My basic field is corporate and financial law. We're in the deals business here—private offerings, and so on—as well as serving as literary agents. Let me tell you, things have been pulled on me—or attempts made to have them pulled on me—in the gentlemanly publishing business that are more venal than *anything* that was ever tried on me in Wall Street. Not to say that there aren't a lot of people in this industry I'd sit down with and shake hands with on a deal and never have a second thought. Not to generalize that it's a lousy business. But not to elevate it above the so-called commercial world, either.''

Janklow attributes much of the success of his agency to the way he and his associates "examine the prevailing situation with a lawyer's fresh eye" and to the way he applies the resulting insights to a business that has a lot to learn about the uses to be made of modern marketing techniques. "One of the reasons we've been successful is that we recognize that the first audience for a book is the publisher rather than the public," he said. "And how much does the publisher really know about the audience he's aiming for? Look at the way things are going. Look at the bookstore chains, like the B. Dalton people. They're determining the size of *printings,* and the reason for that is that they know more about the business than most publishers do. Self-fulfilling prophecies play a large part in book publishing. What makes a publisher decide that a first printing should be a hundred thousand copies rather than sixty-five thousand? If a publisher buys a book for five thousand dollars, it'll be a *miracle* if anything happens to it. Because in the mind of the publisher it has already failed. But it doesn't have to be that way. We were brought in to help out on a book after the manuscript had been sold to a hardcover publisher for seven thousand dollars. We were asked to see what we could do to save the book from the fate of a tiny sale. We interested Jill Clayburgh in the book, and then, because she was interested, we were able to sell the movie rights with the idea that it would be made into a movie starring Jill Clayburgh. And then, with that movie sale, we went back and got a five-hundred-and-sixty-thousand-dollar offer for the paperback rights. And now it's a *giant* book in the publisher's mind. And when Dalton calls up the hardcover publisher and says, 'We've read this new book and we want to order five thousand, ten thousand copies initially,' the publishers are hysterical, saying, 'We've got a giant book on our hands!' They've had outside confirmation! They feel they *need* someone to tell them they've got great judgment. They *need* to have the *Ladies' Home Journal* say they'll buy the serial rights.

"That's the way the publishers think. There's no marketing input, or, if there is some, it's not extensive enough. You know how they set a printing for a novel? They sit around at the publishing house and a guy says, 'I don't know—fifty thousand?' 'Sounds like a hell of a lot.' 'How many do you think?' 'Oh, I think that booksellers might take five thousand initially.' That's the way they make decisions. Does anybody sit down and put a computer on and see what novels in this genre have done in the Midwest in the past three years? No! They *will!* They'll be doing it very soon. People like me are demanding print guarantees in an author's contract. I want to know how many books are going to be in that first printing. I want to know just what the advertising budget is going to be. And I intend to see that every part of the entire operation, including the sale or licensing of every subsidiary right—paperback, television, movies, overseas rights—will key in to every other part, in an over-all marketing scheme. We *orchestrate* the use of these rights and how they are going to relate to one another. The day I finish a deal, every part of that transaction is a symphony, and every single segment has to play on key and in time. Take our representation of *Linda Goodman's Love Signs.* I went to Europe just for the purpose of auctioning off the foreign rights to *Love Signs.* We got a monumental price for them. That then keyed in to my auction here of the paperback rights, for which Fawcett paid two and a quarter million dollars. The auction keyed in to a huge price that the *Ladies' Home Journal* paid for the serial rights to *Love Signs,* with full front-cover treatment. All this was part of the orchestration to make *Love Signs* the giant book it became.''

To orchestrate the promotion of a book properly, Janklow believes, one needs the kind of information that only research can provide. ''Too many decisions in publishing are just seat-of-the-pants decisions,'' he went on. ''Colgate, for Christ's sake, won't *think* of introducing a new toothpaste without finding out things like 'Do people like mint?' and 'Do they like green? Or is green an offputting color?' Look. Judith Krantz's *Scruples* came along. When I saw the manuscript, I knew instantly what I had. I *knew* it was going to become the No. 1 best-seller. Before its publication, along came *Cosmopolitan,* saying, 'We'll pay you an enormous amount of money for the rights to a sixty-thousand-word condensation of the book, and give you two successive covers of the magazine—one prior to publication, the other right on publication date.' Everybody was extremely excited. The publisher thought it was incredible, unprecedented. I was sitting here without research. Research input would have helped here. But I reasoned that the *Cosmopolitan* audience was a terrific book-buying audience for *Scruples.* So I said no. The consternation that this created I can't tell you. Then I said to the magazine, 'We have a chapter that's a wonderful *teaser.* People who read that in the magazine will really want to read the book. So I'll give you that for a much smaller amount of money and only one cover play.'

''But I go to a big book publisher and say, 'You've got millions. Do this kind of research.' They say, 'You don't understand. Every book is different. It's not like soap.' That's the ego need of guys with master's degrees in English, trying to separate themselves from the world of commerce. Guys who for some reason think the world of commerce is wrong, bent, and the world of literature is terrific. Never mind if they kill you in the contract terms! And any author who signs a standard contract agreement submitted by a publisher is like a tenant who signs a landlord's lease in New York City—if the elevator stops, the heat goes off, your obligation to pay the rent goes *on*. That's what a publisher's agreement is to a writer. And these publishers are the people who want you to think they're above the world of commerce! Marketing is a science. It's not an abstract art anymore. Why not learn some things from it? The conglomerates understand the need for research, for efficient marketing techniques. I can see a situation where whoever is assigned on the conglomerate level to oversee a trade-book company—a guy who isn't filled in with a history of everything that's been done since the invention of movable type—says, 'Listen, I see where you got forty thousand dollars for the book-club rights to that book from the Literary Guild. Good enough, as far as it goes, but how many sales at a greater profit per book is that going to cost us in the bookstores?' Answer: 'I dunno.' They don't know anything. He says, 'Find out. Let's talk about that at the next board meeting.' All of a sudden, you have people scurrying around trying to find answers. Terrific! Dick Snyder, of Simon & Schuster, could go up to the board meeting at Gulf & Western, and he could see the budgetary and cost analysis being done in the big Dominican sugar company that Gulf & Western also owns, and he might say to himself, 'I can use the computer that way. Why don't we have my computer analyze the returns on books—where are they all coming from, and in what patterns?' This being practically the only business in which the retailer can return his merchandise to the wholesaler or publisher for full credit. It's wild! Unbelievable! Once in a while, with a certain kind of book club, we'll make a deal in which books are not returnable.

It's a big advantage. Why do you think the publishers send so many authors to bookstores in a town to autograph books till their arm falls off? I ran into Colleen McCullough out of town. She told me she was autographing between two thousand and three thousand copies of her book a day until she realized why the publishers wanted her to do this— autographed books aren't returnable to the publisher for credit. An amateurishly run business in terms of marketing analysis. We want to encourage efficiency, and we think we're doing it in the way we represent authors and make deals. We don't look upon ourselves as publishers' adversaries. I remember one publisher who had a sampler on the wall behind his desk with a text that read, 'An agent is to a publisher what a knife is to a throat.' But I just want to know what's going to be done with my clients' books, and I want proper control, starting on the most mundane level— consent rights over publicity, advertising, the minimum number of books that are going to go into the stores. And control over all subsidiary rights. The publishers can't sell the Swedish rights without coming to me. They can't design a jacket without coming to me. In the beginning, our requirements caused a tremendous amount of resentment on the part of publishers. But we say to the publishers, 'Look, once you've bought our book, our interests are identical. We'd like to have a proper input. We'd like to tell you what we think can be helpful.' Some publishers have learned to work very closely with us. And we turn away an incredible number of projects.''

CHAPTER **6**

Hollywood:
''The Deal Fabric''

ALTHOUGH Morton Janklow has achieved considerable renown as a lawyer-agent and as an innovator in his field, he is by no means alone in seeking to obtain some measure of control over, or participation in, every important decision connected with the publication of a book whose author he represents. ''Orchestration'' is a word that has also been entering the language of certain other composers of big publishing deals—people who for the most part happen to center their activities in Hollywood rather than New York.

The already complicated relationships that now exist among hardcover publishers, mass-market book publishers, and the chain bookstores under the stimuli of conglomerate money, big-time literary agentry, and coast-to-coast television promotion in the endless race for blockbusters have been rendered even more complicated by the increasingly close involvement of the motion-picture industry with the publishing business. In general, this involvement has coincided with a trend over the past decade or more toward conglomerates' acquisition of motion-picture companies along with book-publishing companies—acquisitions that have made Gulf & Western, which was originally a manufacturer of auto parts, also the owner of Paramount Pictures and of Simon & Schuster and Pocket Books; made Warner Communications, which is a major producer of films and records and the part owner of the third-largest cable-TV system in the country, also the owner of Warner Books; and made MCA, which is the owner of Universal Pictures, also the owner of the hardcover publishing houses G. P. Putnam's Sons, Richard Marek, and Coward, McCann & Geoghegan, and the paperback houses Berkley Publishing and Jove Publications. Though the traffic between the motion-picture and book-publishing arms of any particular conglomerate may not in practice have produced the kind of competitive advantage envisioned by some of the principals when the mergers were taking place—the notion, for example, that conglomerates might dominate their competition by allowing their wholly owned divisions to favor each other in trade, with a hardcover-publishing division regularly giving the paperback division and the motion-picture division the inside track on the subsidiary rights to its published works—conglomerate ownership of motion-picture and publishing companies has certainly helped create an atmosphere in which books, movies, and television programs can be regarded as integrated components of a total commodity. "In a certain sense, we are the software of the television and movie media," Richard Snyder, the president of Simon & Schuster, declared some time ago in discussing trends in the publishing business. What has developed now is a situation in which books, movies, and television programs together may be considered the software of multimedia packages.

The shift in the balance of power from the hardcover houses to the mass-market-paperback houses, together with the increased influence of some agents, was viewed cautiously within the motion-picture industry, which had seen, since the Second World War, the break-up of the major studios and their near-total control over actors and directors and over all kinds of theatrical-distribution and other rights, and had seen the rise of new varieties of deal-makers— independent producers as well as directors, big-time Hollywood agents, and packagers. The practice of putting together complicated deals had so quickly become natural to the Hollywood style that when the West Coast operators witnessed the upheavals in the publishing business it was not long before they began moving into the book business as active participants. Their principal contribution was the tie-in—a new kind of speculative amalgam, involving hardcover and mass-market-paperback books and high-pressure advertising and television as well as motion pictures themselves.

In the tie-in, the traditional process whereby the movie rights to books published by hardcover houses were sold to Hollywood movie companies has been supplemented by another process, in which the Hollywood people act as far more than the buyers of rights; under a kind of prearranged joint venture, the publication of a particular mass-market paperback may be tied in with the release of a movie bearing the same title. Another kind of scheme has been put to use, in which the producers of a movie have their own book version of a movie prepared, and then license the book-publication rights of this "novelization" to paperback, and even to hardcover, publishers as part of a package.

Probably the first instance of this reverse order of things, in which the content of a movie was subsequently converted into book form, was a "book treatment" manuscript that the publicity department of R.K.O. Pictures concocted in 1932 and arranged to have published in book form to celebrate the forthcoming movie "King Kong." The word "novelization" to describe the movie-to-book process has been employed in Hollywood since the nineteen-sixties. An example of the formal use in a legal document occurred in

1976, thirty-seven years after M-G-M released David O. Selznick's production of the movie version of Margaret Mitchell's *Gone with the Wind*. According to the producer David Brown, who is an associate of Richard D. Zanuck, in the Zanuck/Brown Company, he and Zanuck entered into negotiations with the Margaret Mitchell estate, on the estate's initiative, for the right to produce a movie that would be a sequel to "Gone with the Wind." In these negotiations, Brown recalled, the executors of the Mitchell estate agreed to sell to the production company the right to license the publication, in a mass-market-paperback edition only, of a book that would be based on the proposed movie sequel, but they insisted that such a book nowhere—in the cover copy or in any promotional text—be described as a "novel." In the resulting contract, Brown said, the two parties came to an accommodation by agreeing that the book could be described as a "novelization" of the movie. Although a script for the sequel and the book version of the script were prepared, the new movie version never got before the cameras, and since the deal with the Mitchell estate was that the book based on the script couldn't be published unless the movie was made, the project never got very far off the ground.

The movie-to-book form took a while to develop commercially. "When I began working with Richard Zanuck, mass-market-paperback reprint rights to screenplays were handled by the lowliest member of the publicity department," Brown said. "They weren't even *sold*—they were given out free to the publishers as a promotion aid for the motion pictures they were adapted from." Lee Rosenberg, a partner in the Hollywood agency of Adams, Ray & Rosenberg, told me recently, "Until five or six years ago, arranging for a book based on a movie was a thing usually regarded with disdain by the movie companies. It was, you know, 'O.K., let's use it. The cover of each copy published gives us another mini-poster for the movie. So let's get the book on the paperback racks and into the supermarkets, so the ladies, when they pay for that brown bag full of groceries, can see the name of the movie—we don't even *care* whether they buy the book or not.' '' Usually, the studio publicity people would have the book version of a script churned out by free-lance writers for a percentage of the royalties from the sale of the book. The result almost always appeared as a mass-market paperback, its publication timed to coincide with the release of the movie. When the studio did charge the paperback publisher for the privilege of printing the adaptation of the script, the sum involved was usually on the order of twenty-five hundred dollars.

These conditions began to change rapidly, however, with the publication, in 1976, of a mass-market paperback called *The Omen,* by David Seltzer. The manuscript for the book had been adapted by Seltzer from the screenplay of a movie of that title which was in production at Twentieth Century-Fox. Seltzer, who had a background as a TV-documentary writer and producer, had sold the screenplay of *The Omen,* a gothic thriller, to Warner Brothers some years before, but Warners hadn't done anything with the script, and it had eventually been acquired by Twentieth Century-Fox. Seltzer's agents—Adams, Ray & Rosenberg, whose partners had become convinced that there was a big commercial future in having scripts adapted and published under license to paperback houses—approached the Twentieth Century-Fox people at that point ("before they knew what they had," as Lee Rosenberg has put it), and obtained their agreement to let the agency have a novelization made of the screenplay as a promotional device for the movie. The agents got this right without payment to the studio. Having persuaded Seltzer to do the novelization himself, they went to the New American Library people and sold the mass-market-paperback rights for an advance of twenty-five thousand dollars and a percentage of whatever royalties the book might produce. Seltzer wrote the book on schedule, and N.A.L. published it shortly after the release of the movie, with the result that, according to Rosenberg, "the book acquired a life of its own and sold three and a half million copies, and everybody suddenly woke up to the value of novelizations." The movie did very well, too, but the Twentieth Century-Fox people resolved never again to give away the book rights to any screenplay they had bought. Within a short time, they and other studios began initiating licensing arrangements for the book rights to movies which promised the studios royalty income and provided for other promotional tie-in arrangements between the book and screen versions. At most of the bigger studios, the business of arranging for book tie-ins was transferred from the publicity department to the merchandising department, where novelization rights were marketed along with rights to manufacture T-shirts, games, puzzles, and other merchandise featuring the title of the movie to be promoted. One or two studios went further, and set up special departments to handle the novelization of screenplays they had bought and planned to produce. The first big studio to do this was Universal, which had come under the conglomerate ownership of MCA. Universal established an entity called the MCA Publishing Division, with Stanley Newman, a vice-president of Universal, as its chief officer. One of the big commercial successes of MCA Publishing was a deal for the novelization in paperback of the screenplay for the Zanuck/Brown production of "Jaws 2." This novelization seems to have borne about the same relation to Peter Benchley's 1974 novel *Jaws* that the Zanuck/Brown project for a novelized sequel to *Gone with the Wind* bore to Margaret Mitchell's book, except that "Jaws 2" actually was novelized, and from an existing script—and when the novelization was published, by Bantam, in 1978, its cover was blazoned with this description of its provenance: "A Completely New Novel by Hank Searls Based on the Screenplay by Howard Sackler and Dorothy Tristan Inspired by Peter Benchley's *Jaws.*" It sold more than three million copies.

Such tie-ins may be arranged directly between studios and publishers, or they may be put together by West Coast agents or independent producers or by a combination of the two. Whatever prospects may be ahead for big-money novelization deals (and such deals are very much subject to the vagaries of the entertainment market), a number of Hollywood producers, agents, and publishers' representatives I talked to indicated that they see a rich future in the increasing interdependence of the book-publishing industry and the motion-picture industry—a relationship in which television (including cable television and pay TV) may also be intimately involved. "The fact that so many publishers and some of the big studios are controlled by conglomerates or other big companies has made a shift in emphasis toward the West inevitable for the publishing industry," George Diskant, a partner in the agency of Ziegler, Diskant, told me a while ago. Michael Ovitz, the president of the Creative Artists Agency, which is one of the most successful of the newer talent agencies in the Los Angeles area, declared that the motion-picture business was "in the middle of the most amazing transition" in its relationship to publishing and television. In Ovitz's opinion, it is becoming increasingly difficult for either the movie industry or the book-publishing business to function separately. Almost everywhere he and his West Coast confreres look, they profess to see evidence of the inevitability of a commingling of the media. In Alex Haley's *Roots,* the publishing, television, and motion-picture people see a striking example not only of how books can affect television but also of how television can affect books and the movie business. On the eight consecutive nights in January of 1977 when "Roots" was shown on

ABC as a mini-series, the programs attracted an audience of well over a hundred million people, and attendance at movie theatres in the country is said to have dropped between forty and fifty per cent. Following the mini-series, sales of the hardcover book, published by Doubleday, rose from about six hundred thousand to a million one hundred thousand within two years. By the beginning of 1979, the combined hardcover and paperback sales of *Roots* had reached nearly six million. Even before that, in 1978, the publishing and movie people had a glimpse of what could happen when an original television series was adapted to book form. In April of that year, NBC ran a mini-series called "Holocaust," and Gerald Green, its author, wrote a novelization of it, under the same title; it sold a million seven hundred thousand copies in paperback.

"The entire game is different," Ovitz told me. "It's not a question of dealing, as an agency, with just television or just motion pictures or just books, or even cable or pay TV, or shooting from the hip in the books-to-media business. Now there are a myriad ways of putting projects together, which is what we do here. We don't operate like traditional literary agents. We represent writers *and* producers *and* directors. We basically develop material that we haven't actually bought. We can put together all the elements for a project and, with the agreement of the principals, sell the result as a package. Or we can auction the work of an author straight to motion pictures or to TV or to books, or to all three. Books and movies, movies and books, books and television, television backward to books—it's never happened this way before. We're putting books together that are predicated on magazine articles, putting books together that are predicated on screenplays, and putting movies together that are predicated on books."

In sum, the aim of such efforts is a multimedia merchandising program in which books, movies, and television programs based on a single work—and all associated promotion—are fused into a coördinated whole, as a packaged "property." Such a package is composed of "elements." A script is an element. So is a writer. So are a book, a producer, an actor or a troupe of actors, a director. In contrast to simpler times, in which it was taken for granted that a published book originated with an author, who conceived a set of ideas on a theme and then developed them in manuscript form, the existence of even an unfinished manuscript may not be a necessary precondition to selling a book for a large sum to a publisher in these multimedia deals, since actual authorship often becomes an ancillary consideration in what I have heard called in Los Angeles "the spontaneous generation of a literary property." This "generation" does not have to take place in the mind of a writer; it can occur around a conference table in the office of a producer or an agent, who may then add to it "elements," including the writer, who is "acquired" sooner or later in the packaging processes. A mutimedia package thus assembled normally involves a sale of the paperback rights for the proposed book to a publishing house, and sometimes both a hardcover and a paperback publication deal. The terms of the deal specify that the publication dates and the promotion of the various editions of the book are to be coördinated with the promotion and release of the movie that is also to be manufactured from the original idea. In the case of the novelization of a screenplay for mass-market-paperback publication, the studio usually owns the logotype of the title shown on the cover of the resulting book and retains the right to control the use of the particular typeface or logo used for the title of the movie both on the screen and in ads in all media, and also retains control over the artwork, and even the colors used in the artwork, shown on the cover of the novelization. "A total manipulation of package" is how one Hollywood executive described it to me.

The essence of such a system is to make the promotion in one medium feed the promotion in another to achieve a maximum marketing effect in both. The sequence may go like this: A book based on the script of a movie yet to be produced or on an idea put forward by either a producer or an agent, or even a writer, is sold to a paperback publisher or to a hardcover publisher, who then sells the reprint rights to a paperback house. The book serves as a device to publicize the forthcoming movie well ahead of its completion and release, and in the meantime the movie company may put money into advertising the book. At the time the movie is released, the book, whose sales may well have passed their peak, embarks on a sort of second life, stimulated by the showing of the movie and by all the advertising attached to it. Since the promotion of the book and the movie are coördinated according to a prearranged program, both the producers and the publishers involved—not to mention the author—stand to gain greatly from the mutual plugging.

For the movie people, this kind of multimedia deal has added advantages. Nowadays, even before book rights are sold, a movie project, once it reaches the production stage, can be advanced at low risk, in comparison to the risks once encountered, through what amounts to the sale of futures on the film in the form of various ancillary rights. "Just the prices obtained for TV use have gone up enormously," Diskant told me. "A movie that sold to TV for one or two million dollars a couple of years ago is now selling for six or seven or eight million, and some movies are selling for as much as twenty million. Those prices are there because the TV networks don't want the pay-TV industry to go out and license all the negatives. When you get a movie project set up, you can sometimes get advances from foreign and domestic distributors and from pay TV, and they can so reduce your risk that often a motion-picture studio can actually be out"—that is, financially in the clear—"before the picture is released. These multimedia rights even extend into the music business. Soundtrack rights have become a vital part of the assets of a movie, and you want to control those from the beginning. Look at the soundtrack album of 'Saturday Night Fever'—for a while, its sales outgrossed those of the movie! Unfortunately, the studio didn't get most of the proceeds of that album, but you can see that in other situations like this whatever benefits you can earn, and at no cost to the producers of the movie, from book-publication rights and through book-movie tie-ins may just put you that much farther ahead."

David Brown agrees with this assessment. "Under the management that you find at big companies like MCA, the marketing and publicity people are a very efficient breed," he told me. "So with the sale of all these ancillary rights, including outside book-publishing rights, the financing and promotion even of what might turn out to be an unsuccessful film represent a very low risk to a studio."

From the point of view of the publishers, the risk tends to be considerably higher, because a book or novelization on which they have advanced substantial sums may not sell, or the movie to which the book is tied in may not be successful. But when the tie-in works, the rewards can be great, and the huge sums that a motion-picture company may budget for advertising and publicity can give an enormous boost to the paperback sales of a tie-in book. "At the time a movie-book deal is made with a paperback publisher," Brown says, "he knows that up to eight million dollars may be spent by the studio on advertising for the film, which is certainly going to redound to the paperback company's advantage, because that title is going to appear not only on the cover of the book but on marquees everywhere and on all the TV commercials for the movie and in print ads all over the United States." Of the attitude of publishers toward the benefits that movie-book tie-ins can confer on them when properly "orchestrated," Ovitz remarked to me, "In the past four or five years, people in the book business have seen many things they had never thought would exist. Not only have they arrived at a point where paperbacks are being advertised and promoted on TV but books are getting exposure just everywhere. The publishers see book tie-ins placed right in the trailers for the movie, they see the books themselves sometimes on special stands in the lobbies of the theatres where the movie is showing, they see waves of publicity about their authors breaking again and again—with the publication of the paperback, the release of the movie, and the new campaigns for the book that are timed to follow this release."

Diskant told me, "Your successful authors have become personalities, and, with the publication of the various editions, your personalities are in all the media. They're all very merchandisable, and the income is such that they can live next to [one of the big stars]. Look at Irving Wallace and that party he threw on his estate, for five or six hundred people, at the time of the last convention of the American Booksellers Association out here. That sort of thing is very rare these days in Hollywood."

Though failures inevitably occur, the proportion of big publishing successes among book-movie deals has been such that over the past few years New York publishers have been establishing offices on the West Coast to get in on the ground floor of movie tie-ins and other multimedia deals. Pocket Books has its own representative in Los Angeles. So have Bantam and Warner Books, and New American Library had one for a while. Hardcover publishers, even though they usually have no control over the disposition of motion-picture rights to the books on their lists, have developed a keen interest in encouraging the sale of those rights, through the authors' agents. "The reason the publishers are extremely interested in having the agents offer these motion-picture rights, and as soon as possible after the manuscript is accepted for publication, is that the sale of these rights jacks up the price for the reprint rights, because it gives the reprinter two shots at the paperback—one before the movie is completed, and the other after it's completed," Brown told me. "Even an early *option* by a motion-picture company on an accepted manuscript has a profound effect on the paperback bidding." The effect of all this is to weave agents, producers, and publishers together in something that one hears referred to as "the deal fabric."

An example of the "generation of a literary property" and how it was wrapped up in a "deal fabric" was outlined to me by Diskant. The process—which involved the Ziegler, Diskant agency; George Englund, an independent producer who has been responsible for, among other films, "The Ugly American;" Paul Erdman, the author of the 1976 novel *The Crash of '79*; the director Sydney Pollack; the hardcover house Simon & Schuster; and the paperback house Pocket Books—was described this way:

"George Englund approached us with an idea. Englund is very close to Clifford Perlman, the chairman of Caesars World. Englund saw him as a great background source for a motion picture about the gambling phenomenon in this country—an important social and economic phenomenon, with gambling stocks becoming some of the hottest stocks on the stock exchange. Englund wanted to discuss with us the possibility of developing a motion picture on this subject. Englund had no beginning, no middle, and no end for the movie, and he had no characters. He had an idea, and he figured that his relationship with Cliff Perlman would provide him with top-level access to the gambling scene all around the country. We thought the idea had great possibilities. A few days later, taking things a step farther, we put Englund in touch with Paul Erdman as a possible writer—after we had explained to Erdman what it was all about. Erdman loved the idea. We discussed with Erdman the possibility of developing the idea as a *book*. He said he'd love to do a book about it. So I told Englund, 'We're planning on making a book deal.' I explained that an author of Erdman's stature would have to have complete autonomy—he'd have to control all the literary rights. Then, early in 1978, I called up Dick Snyder, of Simon & Schuster, who's Erdman's publisher and did a very good job in promoting *The Crash of '79*. I said, 'Dick, I've got a great idea.' I told him about Englund's approach and what the subject of the movie would be. I said, 'We've got the producer; I want to get an important director involved, and an important writer. I want this to start with a book. I want to have it published even before the screenplay might be completed. I want the book to be a publishing event on its own. I've got the author to agree to consult with the screenwriter while the book is being written.' Dick reacted to the project with enthusiasm. I had Erdman prepare a two-page outline of what the book would deal with. It would be called *Atlantic City*. After a few months, on the basis of conversations between Dick and me, and Erdman's outline, Dick agreed to publish the book under our terms. In June of 1978, Simon & Schuster agreed to a seven-figure advance—a *hard* seven-figure advance. Dick gave me some advice about the project. I sat down with the producer, and our next step, in April or May of 1979, was to bring in Sydney Pollack as director—Sydney happens to be a client of mine.

"All the details of the book-movie deal were spelled out in the contract with Simon & Schuster. It's a hardcover-paperback deal, with Pocket Books—which, of course, is owned by Simon & Schuster—doing the paperback. The author will earn royalties of fifteen per cent from *both* editions. He doesn't share them. And he retains all ancillary rights. It's important for the agent to control all the markets that an author's book is going to be in—foreign translations, television, video cassettes, motion pictures, hardcover, paperback, what have you. And that's also important to Erdman, who is very sophisticated about these things. As for us as agents, we make sure that we not only control all the markets but *choreograph* their interplay. You want the hardcover coming out at a certain time. Then you want the paperback out at a properly calculated time. This movie will probably cost fifteen million dollars to make. We had to find a partner to finance and distribute the movie. For this, we went to Warner Brothers, and in late spring of 1979 we made a deal. The next step was to hire screenwriters. Paul is working on the book now. He's also feeding his manuscript to the screenwriters as he turns it out. If all goes according to schedule, the hardcover version of the book will be published in 1981. Filming of the movie will probably start at the same time. Then will come the first paperback edition. It'll be presented as a *true* paperback edition rather than as a tie-in with the movie. During this time, the hardcover and paperback editions will be getting all the visibility; they will be building interest, and an audience for the motion picture that is being made. By the time shooting is finished and the movie is edited and ready to show, the paperback edition of the book should have been out for three months or so. The paperback will have had the benefit of an enormous amount of publicity and advertising money in print and on TV, and it's probable that the movie studio will contribute to the publisher's advertising appropriation for the hardcover book, too, and undoubtedly Erdman will be making TV appearances all over for the hardcover and paperback editions. Then, after the paperback has been out those three months and the movie is released, a *new* paperback edition of the book, with a new cover, explicitly tying the book in to the movie, and bearing the movie artwork and logo, will be published. And that will set off a new round of publicity, promotion, and advertising." And perhaps a new round of TV appearances by the author, too.

CHAPTER 7

Tie-In Business

A PERFECT ILLUSTRATION of Richard Snyder's dictum about the book business being the software of the entertainment industry, the *Atlantic City* project also serves to illustrate the difference between the approaches used in what one could consider an older era of "publicity" and a newer era of "hype." Up to now, publicity—intense publicity—concerned itself essentially with affairs of the moment. But the idea of hype implies something more than mere publicity. It implies not one event but a series of events (or pseudo-events), each of which is calculated to interact with, and heighten the effect of, the next one. And it seems that hype—as it applies to modern multimedia promotion and merchandising, at least—tends to take on even greater force than what it purports to help bring about. It's a kind of symbolic overdrive, to which the customary gears in the promotional machine become subordinated. With hype, a hardcover book, say, may be heralded as an event, but when the time for the event arrives, and sometimes even before it arrives, the significance of the event quickly declines, because the significance lies not in the event itself but in its precursive and interactive function as part of a series—the hardcover, the author's TV appearances, the big auction, the paperback, the movie, the paperback-movie tie-in, the TV spinoff, and so on. With hype, it's the shadow of expectation concerning some subsequent step in the series—the sense of what's-coming-next—that somehow seems to assume greater substance than the event that has just materialized. "Soon to be a major motion picture"—that is not only hype for some future film version of a book but also a shadow intended to confer a strange kind of reality, or "credibility," on the book itself. And this situation has a corollary in which the book is a shadow and some future movie the reality. One Los Angeles agent, speaking of his efforts to "shepherd and orchestrate the literary and creative evolution of a property" that was based on an idea being developed by his agency for a movie, told me that, having "acquired" a writer, he was proposing a hardcover-paperback deal with a New York publisher in order to "get credibility" for the acquired writer and for the eventual paperback edition of the book itself, which, if it was successful, would serve as "an exploitation device" for the proposed movie.

One of the first of the big mass-market-paperback houses to establish a representative in Los Angeles to specialize in acquiring movie novelizations and arranging movie-book tie-ins was Bantam Books, and in the last couple of years or so Bantam has broadened its participation in the movie business. At last year's convention of the American Booksellers Association, in Los Angeles, Marc Jaffe, then the president and publisher of Bantam (he subsequently left Bantam, and became executive vice-president of Random House and executive vice-president and editor-in-chief of Ballantine Books), informed a discussion group that his company was adopting "a whole new way of working with films." This, he said, was a scheme whereby Bantam editors would enter into what he called "a co-creative" relationship with producers or agents; that is, the editors would sit down with these people to "generate" ideas for book-movie combinations.

Bantam's principal West Coast representative concerned with such matters is Charles B. Bloch, who directs a wholly owned Bantam subsidiary in Los Angeles called Entertainment Discoveries, Inc. E.D.I. was formed in 1977, Bloch told me, as the result of a growing conviction among the Bantam people that, "with the proliferation of all these mergers in which motion-picture companies and book-publishing houses were involved," it would be advisable for Bantam—which is under the ownership of the Bertelsmann publishing empire, in Germany, and has no conglomerate connections in the United States—to take steps on its own to develop a closer relationship with the movie industry. E.D.I. is set up as a movie-production company, with Bloch as the executive producer. Bloch not only arranges with studios or various independent producers or agents for novelizations of screenplays which will be published by Bantam as tie-ins to the movies to be made from those screenplays but also arranges joint ventures in which Bantam may actually co-finance the writing of screenplays in conjunction with certain Bantam books; in effect, that is, Bloch hires the scriptwriters for E.D.I. in addition to signing up the authors of the Bantam books dealing with the same subject matter. In part, this new step seems to have arisen out of Bantam's reaction to the constantly rising prices being paid to hardcover houses by paperback publishers—because of which, Bloch told me, "we have been developing our own original books, which we have acquired full basic rights to, so that we are not only publishing the originals in paperback but also making these reverse deals by licensing the hardcover rights to them to hardcover publishers almost every month." Bloch describes this increasingly common practice as "our protection against the OPEC of the hardcover publishers." Once Bantam had initiated this practice, Bloch told me, it seemed natural, in view of the firm's parallel involvement in the movie-book tie-in business, to get actively involved in the movie business as well.

The first feature film developed through the efforts of E.D.I. and Bantam was "The Fog," a horror film that was released in February, 1980. The project began with a two-page outline for a screenplay which had been prepared by two scriptwriters, John Carpenter and Debra Hill, and had come to Bloch's attention. Bloch sent the outline on to Jaffe, at Bantam, and as a result, according to Bloch, "we selected the property for development as a book and as a motion picture, and E.D.I. financed the writing of the screenplay, while Bantam financed the writing of the book." Bloch became the executive producer of the film, which was eventually produced by Debra Hill. Financed and distributed by Avco-Embassy Pictures, "The Fog" was released in neat synchronization with the publication of Bantam's paperback ("The Terror-Filled Novel THE FOG, by Dennis Etchison, Based on a Motion Picture Written by John Carpenter and Debra Hill"), and, of course, the promotion of the book was helped along by lavish advertising for the movie. By October, 1980, the sales of the book were above three hundred thousand. As for the movie, Bloch declared that it is expected to gross thirty million dollars in box-office receipts worldwide. And Bantam, which has a guaranteed share of the movie profits coming to it, will eventually be a major beneficiary of the movie venture as well as of the book publication.

Another Bantam-E.D.I. project involved a film called "The Iron Mistress of Malibu," which began as a movie script that was owned by an independent producer, Stanford Blum, and had been submitted to Orion Productions but, according to Bloch, was not found to be "shootable" as a motion picture by the Orion people. To convert the script into something shootable, Bloch made an arrangement with

Marcia Nasatir, a producer for Orion who had formerly been an editor at Bantam, whereby Bantam paid a writer, Barry Kaplan, to adapt the script for publication as a "true" book rather than a tie-in. At the same time, E.D.I. entered into an agreement with Orion and with Stanford Blum under which the original screenplay of "The Iron Mistress of Malibu" would be discarded and another screenwriter would adapt the Bantam novel—when that was completed—as a new screenplay. The movie would be produced by Blum and Marcia Nasatir. "It seems like a tortuous way to go," Bloch conceded in discussing the project with me. But, he added, "it also seems that there aren't any simple deals anymore."

Other paperback publishing houses are trying to set up similar joint-venture arrangements, in which they obtain, in effect, a proprietary interest in movie productions, but such efforts by publishers are not confined to the mass-market-paperback people. Some hardcover publishing houses are also attempting to make book-movie deals based on the "co-creative" development of ideas for books and movies, with the hardcover publishers putting up some kind of financial stake, which, they calculate, is worth risking because of the handsome payoff in box-office as well as book sales if the movie part of the deal goes forward. "Moving for the most part in a very quiet way, hardcover publishers are developing motion-picture material," one Hollywood agent told me. "An author comes to them with an idea that the hardcover publishers think smells theatrical, and soon the publishers are in there trying to put a movie-book-development deal together." When I asked Michael Ovitz about this, he said there was no question about the reality of the trend. "These hardcover publishers want to be equity partners in motion pictures," he said. "They feel that if they get into the development process at an early enough stage, they can wind up retaining a major equity position in motion-picture rights to certain books. All the publishers are on the lookout now for that nine-million-dollar movie that will gross two hundred million dollars—on the lookout for the hot script that'll be next year's runaway hit movie, so the publishers can control the rights to the paperback tie-in. And some of them are trying to get in on the ground floor by also doing a hardcover on the material for the movie, so they can get control of the paperback rights in anticipation of the movie-tie-in edition.''

One representative of the hardcover industry who is actively on the lookout where Hollywood is concerned—and is not so quiet about it—is David Obst, the president of Simon & Schuster Productions. Obst, a brisk and bearded man of thirty-four, got into publishing by becoming an agent in Washington, D.C., where he scored a big success by representing Bob Woodward and Carl Bernstein in the sale of their books *All the President's Men* and *The Final Days*, and also in the sale to Robert Redford's production company of the movie rights to *All the President's Men*. Soon after making those sales, Obst moved to Random House and then to Simon & Schuster, where he had his own imprint. He is enthusiastic about the potential rewards of strengthening the connection between Simon & Schuster's publishing activities and the movie industry, and to pursue this course he moved out to Los Angeles. I had a talk with him just before he made the migration.

"What's happening is that East Coast editors and publishers have been going out to the West Coast and spending a week or ten days at a time there, staying at the Beverly Hills Hotel, calling on all the same people at the studios, cherry-picking what's available, and bringing it home with them," Obst told me. "I learned, having come into the publishing business in Washington, that you had to be on the scene to know who the potentially successful writers were. I'm gambling on the theory that there is intelligent life on the West Coast. Which I can develop in book projects. Projects for which I can come up with original story ideas and find authors capable of working with them. Projects having spectacular rights potential. When something like this works, it's very lucrative, because the film companies are so hungry for material. They're willing to buy for enormous sums of money the rights to books that we can develop, and, more important, they're willing to put their resources into breaking these books further into the public consciousness through advertising dollars and promotion.

"One thing I've learned from being an agent is that to get people to pay attention to a book you have to hit them in the media. Take *The Final Days*—we broke that on the cover of *Newsweek* as a hard-news story, and the book just *flew* out of the stores. I've always contended that in order to make a book work you have to have the public hear about it at least five times in three days, through the news or ads or word-of-mouth, or all three. Books and movies feed off each other. And in the financing, too. When the book is bought for hardcover and the rights are sold to a reprint house, the reprinter knows that he may have two shots at the market, the second being a movie tie-in if a movie is really made. And in the meantime there has been such a financial commitment by the studio that has entered into a book-movie deal that the chances of the book's actually becoming a movie may well be greater than they would be otherwise. Then, of course, if the movie actually is completed, the reprinter has his second chance to recoup with a tie-in edition.

"I want to develop properties through which talented screenwriters would be given an opportunity to write in a different medium. There's an economic need for this. What you're dealing with in publishing, fundamentally, is a limited and shrinking pool of talent that is being bid for by an expanding group of conglomerates, so the prices for acquisitions are going through the roof. I hope to come up with new rules that will encourage talented screenwriters to write books. The kind of people I'm talking about normally get six figures to write a screenplay. For a publisher, six figures as an advance for a first novel is just too high; the kind of money these screenwriters are used to is not normally there in publishing to entice them. So I've worked out formulas to make it possible for them to be enticed."

Essentially, the formulas consist of joint-venture arrangements between Simon & Schuster, the screenwriters, and studios interested in producing movies that are based on scripts written on the same theme as the book manuscript paid for by Simon & Schuster. Obst explained, "I go to the studio and get the people there to put up seventy-five thousand dollars, I put up seventy-five thousand, and I develop the book, and when it's finished and if it's terrific, I get the studio enthusiastically behind it—and with that I go out to the reprinters and sell the reprint rights."

Or, instead of approaching a writer first, Obst can begin with a conference with a producer during which, again, there occurs a "spontaneous generation of a literary property." One such conference involved Obst and Peter Guber, who produced the movies "The Deep" and "Midnight Express" for Casablanca Film Works. "Peter is one of the best promoters in the business," Obst said. "Peter and I were sitting around one day outside his house, talking about books and movies we could do together. Peter lives up on Mulholland Drive, overlooking the city. He said, looking down on the city, 'What would happen if all this burned down?' I said, 'There would be a terrible L.A. fire. Let's do the terrible L.A. fire as a book and as a movie.' So all right. So I found a writer, and we came up with a concept, and Peter and I came up with a story line, and we gave it to the writer, and the writer wrote the book. It was O.K.—

we did have revisions on it." The book, which was written by Edward Stewart, was called *The Great Los Angeles Fire*. Simon & Schuster has published it in hardcover. Obst went on, "And because Peter is such a good promoter we took the project to Columbia Pictures, and because of Peter's track record of having two enormous successes as a producer the studio bought a share of the book rights and the movie rights to the book for more than ten times what we'd had to pay the author. Then, because we'd made this big movie sale, we went to Fawcett, and Fawcett gave us a six-figure advance for the paperback rights.

"We did something innovative in selling the paperback rights. In addition to sending the book around to all the paperback houses, we produced a five-minute video cassette about *The Great Los Angeles Fire*. What it was was L.A.-TV-station outtakes with voice track over it taken from the book, and it was like this stirring five-minute movie, and at the end, coming out of the flames, was a copy of the book. Peter's just a genius at that sort of thing. And we got a book that if we'd done under normal circumstances"—that is, only as a book—"would have had a mediocre life, but now it's almost an assured success, because we're close to four hundred thousand dollars in sub-rights sales on it before we've even published it. We gave the author a thirty-thousand-dollar advance to write the book, and Peter's risk was only ten thousand dollars, as his part of the author's fee. This is an example of almost-no-risk publishing."

CHAPTER **8**

"Non-Traditional Methods"

T HE CHANGES that have beset book publishing over the last two decades have inevitably created considerable turmoil among those who work in trade-book publishing. This turmoil is evident in the shifting of editors and authors from publishing house to publishing house in search of more secure or more advantageous arrangements; in changes in the traditional role of many trade-book editors, and also in the editorial process itself; in changes in the kind of people who enter publishing or who seem to be on the ascendant in the business; in what many editors feel is undue pressure on them to produce highly promotable books; in changes in the basic quality of competition between publishers, with complaints by the few remaining independent trade-book publishers that they are having trouble holding their own in a conglomerate-dominated business; in difficulties that certain categories of published authors are encountering in having their works kept in print and in the bookstores; and in the serious problems that some authors appear to have in getting their works published at all.

The infusion of large amounts of corporate money into book publishing in the nineteen-sixties and seventies was bound to mean that many publishing houses could not be run as they once were—in the business sense, at least. In contributing not only large pools of money but also centralized and highly computerized systems of accounting and inventory control to an industry that in many ways was antiquated and inefficient, the conglomerates wanted to turn the publishing houses they had taken on into financially rational structures. To this end, they commonly imposed long-range financial-planning programs and profit goals on the houses they acquired. But although it was clearly in the interests of the acquired publishers to provide, in their financial planning, for future expansion and for certain long-range publishing programs, such as a projected series of books requiring large outlays of money, there were areas of trade-book publishing in which any attempt to plan was bound to be futile. No matter how readily a sort of profit-quota approach might be imposed by conglomerates on, say, their manufacturing divisions—and that is often done in a ruthless manner—trade-book publishing tends not to be amenable to such programming, for it is inclined to be very much of a variable, up-and-down business from year to year. Alan D. Williams, the vice-president and editorial director of Viking-Penguin, Inc. (which is now owned by Penguin Books, which, in turn, is owned by the British conglomerate known as the Pearson-Longman group), observed to me, "One of the most unpleasant fallouts from some of the conglomerate operations is the devotion to budgeting. It's true that in the past too many trade-book publishers were operating without budgeting of a rational sort. But the expectation of some conglomerateur that as a trade-book publisher you can sit down and project five years of sales is really absurd. To do so, you would have to count on the works of authors whom you might not even know about, on the output of people who are in the process of being discovered or who are busy writing books whose artistic and commercial worth you couldn't even estimate for another two or three years." Aaron Asher, the editor-in-chief of Farrar, Straus & Giroux, which is one of the few independent trade houses left, says of trade-book publishing, "It's a business that even when it's well run still shows jagged peaks and valleys in its financial statements. It drives the broker types, the business types, crazy. Because what they teach you in the Harvard Business School is that if you merge a company properly and plan it properly, with five-year plans and all the rest, your curve is going to go like *that*." He made an upward-sloping gesture with his arm. "One of the things that have continued to astonish me is how little sophistication about this business there is among outsiders."

At any rate, the gap between the desires of the conglomerate owners and the recalcitrant nature of the publishing business was bound to create certain fundamental pressures on the financial officers of the acquired publishing houses, and a sense of such pressures was bound to filter out into editorial departments. The conglomerate owners felt, of course, that what they wanted was quite reasonable. They had paid large sums to acquire the publishing houses, and that money was supposed to be recouped, and recouped again, in an orderly way. Given the vast resources of the conglomerates and their experience with and understanding of modern merchandising techniques, a determined program of seeking out, buying, and promoting best-sellers seemed to be the surest way for the acquired companies to exert their new economic clout and capture dominant shares in the trade-book market. And the publishers themselves were eager to use the resources of their owners to buy as many winners as possible in the best-seller sweepstakes. As Ronald Busch, who was once at Ballantine and is now president of Pocket Books, was quoted as saying, "With all the conglomerate money in publishing today, it's like playing Monopoly."

The consequences of this approach—notably including the headlong pursuit of best-sellers, which has become a controlling force in book publishing—could only be far-reaching. One of the most noticeable effects has been that in respect to editors the management of publishing houses has tended to place more and more emphasis on their ability to seek out and buy publication and subsidiary rights to potential best-sellers; that is, editors have tended to be regarded primarily as acquirers of literary properties rather than as editors per se. Parallel to this new emphasis has been a change in the organizational standing of the subsidiary-rights department. In many publishing houses today, the subsidiary-rights directors, who negotiate and auction off paperback, book-club, and other rights of acquired works, seem to have attained the kind of prestige and authority that were once possessed by experienced editors. And rising in status along with the subsidiary-rights people are the marketing people, the promotion and publicity people, and the advertising people, all of whom may work to promote a book not simply in order to help hardcover sales but to use the resulting publicity and commotion as leverage toward getting a large price for the paperback rights. And then there are the business-oriented people who have been entering publishing in increasing numbers since the conglomerates took over much of the industry—the cost-accounting specialists and the inventory-control managers, whose computer-system formulas apportion and control the use of scores of thousands of cubic feet of book-storage space in warehouses, and whose calculations seem to be increasingly heeded in the process of determining which books can most profitably be kept in stock. And, inevitably, along with these organizational developments there has been a growth of internal review-committee systems, which in many publishing houses has had the effect of diffusing certain literary responsibilities that used to be assumed directly by editors, and of tempering their judgment concerning literary matters.

These things may not have happened to the same degree in all the publishing houses acquired by conglomerates, but they have happened in enough of them to create widespread changes in publishing. One general effect of such changes has been to polarize the people in the business into groups that might be roughly characterized as the corporate entrepreneurs and the littérateurs. The entrepreneurs are unabashed advocates of the new departures in publishing which have been associated with the era of the conglomerates, and they certainly do not view themselves as the yahoos that their most vehement critics have made them out to be. Their outlook has an ideological tinge. They tend to see themselves as Young Turks fighting against the backwardness of the literary establishment, and as literary populists and innovators who are bringing books to the people on a previously undreamed-of scale, and to attain such a desirable end they are unafraid to use as their means the techniques of modern merchandising, publicity, and multimedia market saturation. Their general attitude is that the publishing business can isolate itself from the mainstream of lively commerce only at its peril.

As for the littérateurs, they tend to see their work as increasingly subjected to the harassments of cost-accounting and cost-benefit calculations, on the one hand, and, on the other, to an ominous emphasis on editors' "performance," which in effect means on their development, promotion, and sale of the big book, of the profit-boosting current best-seller, at the cost of their concerning themselves, as they feel they should, with the discovery and nurturing of perhaps less profitable but artistically more meritorious works. As things now stand, the forces of the entrepreneurs are clearly in the ascendant, but the conflict between them and the littérateurs has brought about a state of great tension within the business. Early in the summer of 1979, this tension was manifested by a controversy that arose over the decision of the Association of American Publishers, in July, to replace their annual National Book Awards, in which meritorious books in seven categories were honored on the basis of recommendations made by a board of writers and book critics, with a new program, to be called the American Book Awards, in which books in seventeen categories, including Westerns, mysteries, and something called "current interest" (this one would include books dealing with "lifestyle, sports, self-improvement"), would be chosen for awards through a process of balloting by publishers, critics, booksellers (including representatives of national chain bookstores), and librarians as well as writers. According to Franklyn L. Rodgers, one of the co-chairmen of the new program, its purpose was to make books "more visible to the public and to reflect their reading interests." The assumption was that the National Book Awards had reflected an élitist attitude toward the tastes of the reading public which was inappropriate to the present circumstances. Reacting to this new method of honoring books, Roger Straus and Aaron Asher, of Farrar, Straus & Giroux, sent off a letter to the co-chairmen of the American Book Awards in which they charged that the new awards "reflect an emphasis on marketing and industry public relations offensive to anyone concerned with the disinterested recognition of literary merit," and that the program promised to be "nothing more than a popularity contest, another ratification of the best-seller lists." Straus and Asher declared that Farrar, Straus & Giroux would submit none of the firm's books for consideration by the new nominating committee.

In August, this letter of protest was followed by another, which had been drafted by the novelist Alison Lurie and signed by forty-four well-known writers and critics, including Nelson Algren, Saul Bellow, Malcolm Cowley, Elizabeth Hardwick, Irving Howe, Elizabeth Janeway, Alfred Kazin, Bernard Malamud, Joyce Carol Oates, Walker Percy, Jay Saunders Redding, Philip Roth, Susan Sontag, William Styron, Wallace Stegner, and Richard Wilbur. The statement charged that awards under the new program were designed to be "a rubber-stamp prize for best-sellers," as a means of insuring that "no more shockingly non-commercial choices," like those by the National Book Awards judges, "are made in the future" and as a device that would "transfer decision-making" concerning the outstanding merit of certain books "from those who write books to those who sell and buy them." The signers called on authors and critics to boycott the forthcoming 1980 American Book Awards ceremonies. But the new awards program committee was undeterred. In October, the American Book Awards people held what was billed as a "marketing-promotion" meeting in the New York headquarters of the Association of American Publishers, at which, according to a subsequent bulletin, such ideas as these were advanced: "creation of an American Book Awards Week;" "use of non-traditional methods and media in order to reach new audiences;" "creation of a seal for both nominated and winning titles;" "the need to reach booksellers early and to have their coöperation and input on marketing ideas;" and "the value of suspense after the nominees have been announced." And, among "non-traditional methods" recommended, "as much exposure on television and radio 'talk' shows as possible should be sought," and, further, "we could consider inviting the public to vote in a 'straw ballot,' with ballots published in local newspapers and a prize for people who guess the winners correctly."

Nominations for the 1980 American Book Awards were announced in February and early March, but in mid-March three authors—Norman Mailer, Philip Roth, and William

Styron—whose novels were among five nominated for awards in the category of hardcover general fiction (nominated against the wishes both of the authors themselves and of their publishers) sent a letter to the Book Awards committee in which they stated that the awards seemed to them to arise out of "commercial and public-relations concerns that should have little to do with the recognition of literary merit," and requested that their books be withdrawn from consideration. The award ceremonies were held on May 1st at the Seventh Regiment Armory, on Park Avenue. According to a subsequent account in *Publishers Weekly*, the prize-giving process involved "an elaborate audiovisual presentation" and, "after a presenter had ripped open the envelope and announced a winner, very much in Academy Award style, a roll of drums."

CHAPTER 9

"All or Nothing" Marketing

T HE GROWING polarization of attitudes within the publishing industry is not always manifested in such dramatic fashion. One difficulty that observers have in trying to catch the spirit of what is going on in publishing is that the idiosyncratic qualities that persist within the business make almost any generalization one might offer subject to important exceptions. Certainly it would be a disservice to the small number of dedicated editors and publishers within the business who have shown themselves determined to maintain their standards of excellence and their encouragement of new writing talent to imply that economic pressures have diminished either their personal force or the value of their contributions to literature. Even within the most seemingly monolithic publishing companies, there are individual editors whose professional skill and energy and devotion to literature are such that they have been able to establish, in effect, their own imprints within those companies. Some of the most notoriously commercial of the houses do publish books of high literary worth, and publish them regularly; and some publishers with the most high-minded of reputations don't hesitate to grab for and publish books whose greatest merit is that they can probably hit the best-seller lists and earn a huge amount of money. Human nature being as unsimple as it is, the conflicting forces of the entrepreneurs and the littérateurs in the publishing business may often turn out to be embodied in the strivings of a single editor or publisher. And perhaps it is the strain that such people undergo in attempting to make simultaneous accommodations with these two forces which accounts for at least some of the prevailing tension among those in trade-book publishing.

The frequent movement of editors from publishing house to publishing house as a result of all the mergers, re-mergers, and acquisitions that have taken place in publishing in the past several years has had a disruptive effect not only on their own professional lives but also on their relationships with the authors they were accustomed to work with, and often on a very intimate kind of understanding concerning artistic matters which may have taken years to arrive at. "A number of my friends in the industry have moved around in four, five, even more houses in the past ten years, during all these conglomerate takeovers," one woman in a trade-book house told me. "Now you have a situation where you have valuable editors who are working in an atmosphere of fear and anxiety and who have been turned to marking up profitable production records instead of spending their time looking for literary excellence. When I started in publishing, during the sixties, the advertising business had that reputation, but now the kind of anxiety we used to associate with advertising has permeated the publishing business itself." And, it seems, the difference between the quality of the pressure felt by an account executive sewing up a new account and a trade-book editor signing up a potential best-seller is steadily diminishing. An extreme example of how things have changed in the once supposedly genteel world of publishing lies in what befell six editors and executives at the publishing house of Harcourt Brace Jovanovich one day in March of 1978. According to an article in *Publishers Weekly,* "Six top people in the general-books department of Harcourt Brace Jovanovich were dismissed suddenly March 20 as William Jovanovich"—the chairman of the publishing conglomerate's board—"announced that he would 'immediately assume direction' of the department. Those fired included Kathy P. Robbins, director of the department since September 1974 and a vice-president of the company, and J. Alan Kahn, whom Robbins had hired last November 1 to serve as editor-in-chief." Others dismissed, according to the article, were the marketing director of the general-books department, the subsidiary-rights director, the general manager, and a senior editor. The article quoted Jovanovich as giving this explanation for the multiple firings: "Over the last eight weeks, the Office of the President and I have been conducting thorough studies, and we are not satisfied with the level of income in relation to outgo. What you spend ought to come back sooner or later. In order to reorganize in a way I thought was sensible, we had to start at the top." The *Publishers Weekly* article said of the people dismissed, "All were told in the morning that they were to be out of their offices by 5 P.M." And according to a report in *Newsweek,* "Guards appeared to supervise the exodus and stand watch at all exits and entrances." While the details of the situation that led to the abrupt editorial dismissals are not public knowledge, one suspects that the performing sea lions at Sea World—the series of marine entertainment parks forming a corporate subsidiary of the Harcourt Brace Jovanovich empire—are accorded more considerate treatment than that.

Of all the questions that have been raised concerning the effects of the big-company, big-book trend in publishing, none have more serious implications than the one having to do with how the present structure of publishing affects works of literary merit which may not be readily marketable by prevailing standards. When editors at hardcover houses are looked upon more as acquirers than as editors, the sheer demands of the acquiring process have obliged many of them to devote far less time than ever before to the actual literary, or even the grammatical, details of their authors' manuscripts, and to the kind of lengthy discussions and constructive reviews of the progress of their literary work which were common not so long ago. Robert Lescher, a literary agent who was formerly an editor at Houghton Mifflin and who is noted for the individual attention that he gives his author clients, says, "You have nowadays a great array of editors of some prowess, who are being well paid, but not really for exercising their editorial skill as such. They certainly have enough of that to talk to an author about his or her manuscript, but they don't really stay with the work once it has been bought. They don't even do the final editing. That's turned over to some anonymous person in the house, whom the author may or may not know." In effect, the continuity of the author's relationship with the person who should be his real editor is disrupted, and his work is thrown into a kind of organizational word-processing machine whose reliability is left to chance. Since the quality of the editing of book manuscripts as well as the quality of the writing itself is a touchstone of a publisher's true dedication to literature, this depersonalization of the editor-author relationship has to be less than auspicious for publishing as a whole.

Aaron Asher, who before coming to Farrar, Straus & Giroux had been an editor at Viking and then was head of the trade-books department at Holt, Rinehart & Winston, expressed his views on the current pressures on editors during a talk I had with him some time ago: "When things were more open in this business, there was a lot more concern and attention paid to the artistic relationship between editors and authors, and, to put it crudely, less talk about deals. A glance at most of the books in bookstores today will reveal that this isn't just nostalgia talking. It's clear that there are now more books appearing that are badly edited and badly written—bad in every aspect, from syntax to structure and internal organization—than there used to be. There has been a definite decline in editorial standards over the past twenty years or so, and it's apparent all up and down the line in the editorial process, beginning with the editor per se and going on through the copyediting and proofreading stages. Perhaps this decline can be connected with a widespread decline of standards in our society. The cause-and-effect relationship is obviously difficult to disentangle, but certainly in publishing the influx of conglomerate money, the increase in the size and pace of publishing operations and in the shifts not only of editors but of authors from house to house, the decreasing loyalties that go with all that, and the whole concept of editorial packaging—all these things tend to distract even the best-intentioned editor from what he used to focus his professional attention on. Not that editors lived in any kind of utopia. Not that editors haven't always been under pressure to produce. You *never* really had time at the office to read and edit as you should. There were so many other things that were part of the editor's job—not only working with agents but worrying about the details of contracts, dealing with authors whose books were published last season, and so on. Reading a manuscript closely or editing it line by line was not something you could ever accomplish properly with a ringing telephone close to you, but now the telephone is going more incessantly than ever. As I say, the pressures were always there, but now they are stronger, because much more money is involved and the big daddy sitting on top is not an Alfred Knopf or a Roger Straus but some anonymous board chairman. You find more and more that editors are people whose title is a misnomer. And you find more and more that as the acquisition of rights has become the primary part of an editor's job, the relationship between the editor and the author has become more limited, with the actual shaping and line-by-line sharpening of the manuscript being relegated to, at best, younger assistants, and in many cases that stage is skipped entirely, with the manuscript going straight into the copyediting phase"—the final editing and styling of the book.

Carol Brandt, whose literary agency, Brandt & Brandt, is one of the oldest and most respected in the business, concurs in the view that the standards of editing, particularly a recognition of the need for internal logic and stylistic consistency in manuscripts, have shown a marked decline in the big-company, big-book era in publishing, along with a general decline in the close relationship and the kind of continued artistic discourse that formerly tended to prevail between editors and authors. Some of this Mrs. Brandt attributes to the constant shuffling of editors from house to house in search of more satisfactory working conditions. "You see such a game of musical chairs going on in book publishing," she said to me. "If an editor comes into a publishing house and hasn't made good in two years—in terms of bringing in profitable books—he's out. There has been just a constant movement of editors. By the time people have gone on to three, or even four, publishers, they've become bruised by the system, and they are no longer truly creative as editors."

Given the preoccupation of publishers and editors with acquiring and promoting best-sellers, and the evident decline in editorial standards, the question of how authors whose works have more literary than commercial promise may fare today is a crucial one in the industry. From what I have been able to observe, apprehension is widespread—among authors, among many agents, among some editors, and even among some heads of conglomerate-owned publishing houses—that in the blockbuster era the artistic worth of many individual authors is being slighted or ignored, and their minimum means of livelihood rendered more precarious than ever.

Many publishers have defended commercially successful works of no great literary merit by saying that the revenues from these helped support, through royalty advances on works in progress, young or beginning writers of talent. This has certainly been true of many of the best-known publishers of serious books. Roger Straus, of Farrar, Straus & Giroux, is known to be such a publisher, and some of the profits derived from best-selling Farrar, Straus authors do, in effect, help support young writers of talent through royalty advances. Moreover, these profits from commercially successful books also help Farrar, Straus to keep publishing such authors, even though their works may sell only modestly over a period of years. Apart from the artistic principle involved, this kind of modest subsidizing is looked upon by the publisher as a long-range investment in people whose work may ultimately turn out to be very profitable.

Of the atmosphere prevailing in most publishing houses, Straus said to me, "Concentration on the big book is at the cost of other books, and this goes contrary to the claim made by publishers who are specializing in the big book—that profits from the big book are used to carry the rest of their lists, the works that aren't going to be big books but, rather, are going to sell *only* four or five thousand copies. I remember a conversation with a younger editor in which he defended the policies of the company he was with—one of the larger companies. He said, 'It's ridiculous to say that we're not interested in books that aren't going to be really big sellers. We're always being told by the publisher to look for books of literary merit.' But then he said, 'Of course, we're told not to bring to any editorial conference any book

that's likely to sell less than four or five thousand copies.'
Well, you can't have it both ways.''

What seems to have happened in publishing in this respect
is that the economic threshold below which an author's
work is considered something that a company just cannot
afford to handle has been raised over the past decade or so
to the point where, in effect, various works of at least some
literary merit that previously would have been published
and then kept in print for a reasonable period are now less
likely to be published at all, and, when they are published,
are much less likely to be kept in print. Inflationary pressures, including high printing costs, have certainly had a
very great deal to do with this trend; still, the few houses—
mostly among the remaining independents—that do continue to publish and keep in print marginally profitable
works of literary merit are subject to at least as many
inflationary pressures as the big, conglomerate-owned
houses are.

The writers of literary worth whose works are most likely
to suffer neglect in the big-company, big-book era fall into
two groups. The first consists of those known in the trade
as "middle authors"—authors who, with one, two, or three
books already published, have committed their professional
lives to writing books but haven't yet met with any great
degree of commercial success. The emphasis on big subsidiary-rights sales—particularly the sale of paperback
rights—has tended to polarize arrangements toward all-or-
nothing transactions, with unfortunate consequences for
some of these authors, and with constricting effects on the
variety of paperback books generally available. Of this situation, Aaron Asher said to me, "If today you go into a
shop that carries a really large selection of mass-market
books, you might still find yourself reasonably happy with
the variety that you see, but not as happy as you might have
been five years ago. And, considering the current rights-

buying patterns, it seems to me that what is going to be available in mass-market paperbacks five years from now will be much narrower in scope than at present. A lot of novels published by front-line quality publishers—by Knopf and Viking, or by us, say—several years ago might have been bought for paperback for a few thousand dollars, or possibly even ten thousand, and might have been distributed perhaps only minimally and available for five or six months, but the authors of those books enjoyed the benefit of having their works, which in hardcover might have sold three thousand copies, in mass distribution in editions of fifty or sixty thousand copies. That's from seventeen to twenty times the hardcover circulation. The publisher and the author shared the money that the reprinter paid. The author got a little money that he wouldn't otherwise have got, and, as for the publisher, the money *he* got from the paperback sale made the difference between loss and break-even on the hardcover edition, and enabled him to go on publishing the writer, or writers like him. Now more and more of these books are not being bought at all by the paperback houses. It's not merely that the mass-market publisher who has laid out a million dollars for a blockbuster can't afford the additional money to buy ten middle books for five thousand dollars apiece—that's a drop in the bucket to him. The *room* isn't there. The investment, the energy, all the thinking in a paperback house are geared to the book that it can make a killing on. Everything else is secondary."

These views are largely shared by a number of agents who make a practice of representing authors of more literary than financial worth as well as those who are commercially successful. Lynn Nesbit, a vice-president at International Creative Management, who is one of these agents, told me, "There's no doubt that, with most of the time and energy of most publishers concentrated on ever fewer but more profitable titles, things are becoming harder for the middle-level book and its author. If they don't happen to be a book-club choice and if it doesn't look as though they'd get paperback money, there's very little chance for them. Some of these authors are still able to sell their books to publishers, but then they find their books are not getting any kind of real in-house support in terms of advertising and so on, and in active interest generally. I just think that the sense of frustration is going to keep building among serious writers who can't get the kind of backing they need."

Miss Nesbit went on, "If, as an agent, you are interested in encouraging serious writing, you have to be careful to represent serious writers who aren't making instant money in addition to representing the more commercial ones. But it is hard under present conditions, and sometimes I get discouraged and wonder if I can afford, not just financially but *emotionally,* to go on doing it. It's such a strain because these authors are suffering so much disappointment—'I've got these wonderful reviews, and why isn't the publisher even advertising the book?' How many times a day can I say, 'Look, you didn't get a big paperback sale.' And they say, 'Well, I would have if they'd advertised more.' It's this *over* and *over* and *over.*"

The all-or-nothing attitude of publishing houses toward books in terms of their sales potential seems to have pervaded the entire system, no matter what personal reservations even the principal officers of large publishing corporations may harbor as to the consequences of such a policy. Oscar Dystel, of Bantam Books, told me, "Everybody in the industry knows that what publishers call the middle novel is suffering. They say you can't sell it. A good story is difficult to sell today. You're dealing with fame, celebrity, hype, as well as with books and authors. You're dealing with 'category books'—mysteries, science-fiction titles, and romantic novels. These historical and romantic novels are just dominating the paperback racks. I think this is an unfortunate development, but retailers who are interested only in fast turnover and immediate profit are concentrating on this kind of retailing. The industry is almost peaking in its concentration on commercial subjects. The penalty is that books of quality and of superior interest are being shoved off the stands. I believe that the public will buy these books if they're exposed to them, but they are being exposed to them less and less. I'm frankly not happy about all this."

"They say you can't sell it"—that is why whole classes of books that may not be really unsalable at all but only unsalable in large numbers are consigned to oblivion in the high-volume, high-turnover system to which so much of the publishing business is now geared. Miss Nesbit said to me, "Most writers never did make much money, of course, but the situation today is that now *some* writers are making enormous amounts of money, and the disparity is greater and more alarming and more frustrating to those writers who aren't. Formerly, authors of middle books *felt* better about themselves, and about the way they were being published, and about their work, than they feel now. They're disheartened by what they see going on in the business. One terrible thing is the big national bookstore chains. This, to me, is perhaps the most lethal part of what's going on, because so far the big publishing houses haven't driven out the smaller publishing houses to the extent that the big-chain-bookstore economy is driving out the personal bookstores, stores in which the people who ran them *cared* about writers and books, and not only best-sellers. And the net effect on publishing of the independent bookstores' going out of business all over is restrictive." In other words, the shrivelling of the independent bookstores as a force in the literary marketplace tends to decrease the demand in the business for those books of literary merit which aren't likely to be of great commercial value to the publisher. And the effect of this situation is that publishers are tending to become ever less willing, as Miss Nesbit says, "to pay any decent kind of money to new writers unless they feel there's going to be an automatic book-club selection."

The second group of authors whose work is increasingly likely to suffer neglect under present conditions consists of authors of first books. Their situation, particularly when they are authors of fiction, is somewhat different from that of the middle authors, in that any publishing house of substance has to continue to publish first authors in order to assure continuity of business. The actual number of first novels being published in hardcover annually does not appear to have changed appreciably since 1970. In the same period, however, the total number of trade books being published has probably doubled, so first novels being put out were obviously not keeping pace with works of nonfiction. Agents say that in general first novels other than works of obvious commercial value have always been difficult to sell to hardcover publishers, and that they are even more difficult to sell nowadays. And when such a first novel is bought, the degree to which it is supported in advertising and so on is usually governed by whether the rights to it are sold to a paperback house, and whether the publishers' salesmen report any interest in it from the big national chain bookstores. But at least from a publisher's point of view there is, as one editor has said, "still room for wishful thinking" about the prospects for the success of a first novel. If that first book doesn't do particularly well in the marketplace, however, the author is likely to encounter substantial difficulty when he offers the publisher a second novel. In the last two or three years, of course, such difficulties have been exacerbated by inflation, which has pushed the cost of producing a book up alarmingly.

The calculations and pressures that have altered almost every aspect of publishing also appear to be having their effect on the question of whether to keep in print books that, while they may not have proved to be great commercial successes, represent the long labors of authors who have manifested some literary talent. Robert Bernstein, the president of Random House, which, together with its Knopf and Pantheon divisions, has a much better record than most publishers in the matter of keeping authors' books in print, says that his company's policy as a rule is to let a book go out of print when its sales have dropped to around two hundred and fifty a year. "The problem is that it now costs so much more to reprint a book," Bernstein told me. "There has been a big change in the physical stocking of books. It used to be much easier for publishers to keep their authors' books in stock, because the manufacturing plants where they were turned out used to stock them free, at least for a reasonable period. Now the plants charge enormous amounts for that. We have to stock *everything* ourselves now. Also, the cost of making small reprints has gone up so much that if you want to order those two hundred and fifty copies to keep up with the demand for a marginal book for a year, you find that you have to order, and be prepared to store, at least a thousand copies—a four-year supply."

But most publishers certainly don't wait for the sales of a book by, say, a middle author to sink to a couple of hundred a year, or anything approaching that figure, before they drop it. Their computerized warehouse systems are geared to keeping book inventories moving, and stocks of a book that isn't selling briskly are likely to be consigned to remainder houses very quickly. Because the entire system—the publishing house itself, the wholesalers, the big chain bookstores, and so on—is oriented toward high turnover, each part of the system accommodates to the other in such a way that books which don't sell in considerable volume tend to have an ever-shorter shelf life. While a certain attrition of titles has always come about naturally in the bookselling process, what the computerized systems have done is to speed the process up to the point where it is brutally peremptory. Quite apart from other considerations, the precious time needed for the work of talented but less commercial authors somehow to seep in among book readers—a sort of decent interval that was made possible in the past by, if nothing else, the traditionally laggard and inefficient nature of the business—has been lost. That is one of those considerations which computerized systems are not programmed to take into account. When I suggested to Oscar Dystel that the inventory-control systems used in book houses to reinforce a big-book policy might cause many talented authors of less swiftly moving books to get lost in the shuffle, his reply was "It's not that they *might* get lost in the shuffle—they *do* get lost in the shuffle. They're the first to go when there's a tightening at any publishing house after a look at its profit-and-loss statements and balance sheets suggests that it has to cut back its business. It's the books that we all want to take a chance on that get put aside."

Regrettable as Dystel finds this situation, neither Bantam nor any other mass-market-paperback house is likely to break out of the existing system. The mass-market publishers, the entrepreneurs, have a different mode of operation. "Publishing a first novel isn't just printing seventy-five hundred copies," Howard Kaminsky, the president and publisher of Warner Books, said to me a while ago. "That's not publishing by the dynamics of the marketplace today. To publish a book is to do more than just print and distribute. Publishing is trying to find an audience for a book. Supporting it, using every means at your disposal. I think we were the first mass-market-paperback house to really *cut back* our list—and our sales have gone up dramatically. Six years ago, we were publishing perhaps twenty books a month. Now we publish perhaps fourteen, including reissues. And our sales are about six times what they were six years ago. We publish *more* books by publishing fewer books.''

On a broader scale, the extent of the impact that the big-book complex in the publishing industry may have on works of literary merit can perhaps be gauged by what has happened to the backlisting of trade books generally. Not many years ago, about sixty per cent of the annual business done by a serious publishing house might come from sales of the firm's backlist—books that the company kept in print. This may still be true of some houses, but the backlisting of trade books as a whole has fallen off so sharply in relation to the sale of current works that, according to Robert Bernstein, the backlist of a publishing house nowadays accounts for only about thirty per cent of its business, "if that." At Random House, part of the gap is filled by the transfer of hardcover titles to trade-paperback form in the well-known Vintage Books series. People at other publishing houses, however, place backlist sales at between fifteen and twenty per cent of the total. In the opinion of Aaron Asher, "the slide of the backlist began about the same time that the subrights tail began wagging the publishing dog." Certainly the extraordinary emphasis that publishers have placed on new big books and the whole complex of multimedia promotion and computerized merchandising have tended to relegate many standard works to the same position of neglect suffered by the works of the hard-pressed middle authors. The merchandising impetus, the multimedia ride just aren't there for backlisted books. As for classic works in hardcover form, it was not long ago that only one hardcover edition of *War and Peace* remained in print in the United States. That was a fairly expensive edition printed by Inner Sanctum, an imprint of Simon & Schuster, and by 1979 even that edition was no longer listed in *Books in Print*. Lately, however, a hardcover edition of *War and Peace* has reappeared in the Modern Library series, which, after being allowed to fade away from bookstore racks in the nineteen-seventies, has been revived by Random House.

But the main consideration in the decline of the backlist in publishing as a whole seems to be corporate cash flow. Acquiring hardcover best-sellers is an expensive business—one in which authors' advances may go into hundreds of thousands of dollars, or, where both hardcover and paperback arrangements are concerned, even into millions. If such large sums were borrowed from outside sources, the publisher would have to pay high interest on them. Selling subsidiary rights to best-sellers probably represents the most efficient way for the hardcover houses to recoup their investment and maintain a high cash flow. In the interests of maintaining that high cash flow, the people in a hardcover house who not many years ago would have been happy to have one or two best-sellers a year now feel that they have to have best-seller after best-seller, all year long. In contrast, any backlisted books that are not in steady and voluminous demand represent to the publishers, by their relatively high inventory and reprint costs, an impediment to large cash flow, since they tend to take a long time to move through the system and realize a financial return. G. Roysce Smith, the executive director of the American Booksellers Association, told me, "Book-publishing accounting procedures assign undue overhead to backlisted books, which have actually earned their money in that their initial production costs have already been paid. This pushes up the cost of backlisted books, and retail booksellers then find they have that much more money tied up in backlist stock lying around in their stores." In recent decisions dealing with the accounting practices of publishers, the Internal Revenue Service has ruled—on the basis of a 1979 Supreme Court decision involving the Thor Power Tool Company—that books held in inventory are not entitled to tax write-downs for depreciated value until after the books have left inventory. The certain effect of this ruling, in which the distinction between inventories of books as repositories of ideas, on the one hand, and stocks of tool parts or the content of manufacturers' warehouses generally, on the other, is ignored, is to offer trade publishers a strong incentive for taking their tax write-downs on existing inventory by simply removing the slower-moving backlisted books, either by remaindering them or by destroying them. When such books are by beginning authors or middle authors, the resulting damage, both artistic and financial, to those authors hardly needs commenting on. The I.R.S. ruling is also certain to discourage publishers from reprinting any current books that they feel may be slow in moving through inventory. The authors are not the only parties injured by this governmental action. As the backlist of books declines generally, increasing harm is certain to befall the independently owned bookstores, whose tradition of rendering personal service by reordering backlisted books has played such an important part in their ability to keep loyal customers. And the more the independent bookstores are harmed (the chain bookstores, whose stake in backlisted books is fairly small anyway, are unlikely to be affected by the I.R.S. ruling), the more the publishing industry is likely to concentrate its efforts on the promotion of the best-selling, fast-moving, cash-flow-producing blockbuster.

CHAPTER **10**

Entrepreneur's View

IT SEEMS REASONABLE to assume that college
people are currently a lot less fervent about publishing as
a career than their counterparts of twenty-five years ago.
It used to be that graduates, entranced by the thought of
working in a profession that had such eminent members as
Maxwell Perkins, and dreaming of how they themselves
might make contributions to the future of American literature, besieged publishers in the hope of obtaining any job,
however badly underpaid, that might be available in some
editorial department. "There aren't that many young people
going into book publishing now," Lynn Nesbit said. "To
become an editor, you have to serve a long apprenticeship,
and for very little money, and fewer young people are willing to do that today. Then, a lot of intelligent, idealistic
young people who otherwise really would be interested in
going into publishing are inclined to say, 'Oh, well, it's such
a bureaucracy. I'm not going to make any money at the
beginning, and I'm going to have to answer to a bureaucracy
in a company that's owned by one of the large conglomerates.' There's a real lack of new literary talent in the
business. Instead, the people who are coming in tend to be

business-minded—people who are likely to fit into a big-company atmosphere.''

David Obst, who might be considered a representative of the West Coast wing of the entrepreneurial cause, agrees that fewer young people are entering publishing, but sees the matter rather differently. In an interview, he told me, "Really bright, ambitious people coming off the campus are not going to be drawn to this business. Few positions are opening, and young people nowadays, especially people who want to develop alternative styles of publishing, can't afford to wait for older people to make way for them. Somebody who is bright and ambitious and who wants to make his fortune in America is not going into publishing. If you look at the publishing business, you see the top positions held by another generation, and, behind that, a real paucity of aggressive, successful, talented editors and publishers coming along. I've never been to a meeting of publishers where they didn't complain about how things are so hard, and how the risks are so great, and how you have to spend money to make money.'' Obst, a risk-taker himself in his role as promoter, deal-maker, and multimedia merchandiser, finds the prevailing situation perhaps even less satisfactory than a Roger Straus, a Carol Brandt, or a Lynn Nesbit does.

The growing state of tension in the business was symbolized at a symposium that was held in January, 1980, on the New York University campus, under the auspices of the PEN-American Center, to discuss the significance of present trends in publishing and was attended by many publishing people, booksellers, authors, and academic people. One of the panelists on the dais was Richard Snyder, of Simon & Schuster, which is perhaps the most commercially successful conglomerate-owned publishing house in the business, and when Snyder, upon being asked to speak, attempted to defend the role of conglomerates in trade pub-

lishing, he was booed by some members of the audience—
a rather sorry commentary on the state of a profession supposedly based on the free circulation of ideas. Snyder's
reaction to this behavior seemed to be one of disdain: he
cut his remarks short. As a member of the audience at the
symposium, I regretted not being able to hear him speak at
length. However, some time before the affair, I had had a
short talk with him at his midtown office. Snyder told me
then that he had just about stopped giving interviews to the
press on the subject of publishing. "I've found reporters
calling me up just to be able to say they'd got me on the
phone," he said. "And not listening to a word I said. Because their stories had in effect already been set up in type.
'The conglomerate story'—what the conglomerates are supposed to be doing to publishing. They'd written their stories
before they ever dialled my number." Snyder went on,
"In an operating sense, I have found no important changes
in publishing because of the conglomerates. In my opinion,
what is really changing the face of publishing in America
is not the conglomerates but the giant book chains. It's not
that as publishers we get the advantage of big accounts with
the chains; it's the fact that the chains serve a different
community of book readers from any that the book business
has ever had before—book readers with different tastes.
The élitism of the book market doesn't exist anymore. A
lot of publishers are having great difficulty dealing with that.
The minute you get into the suburbs, where ninety per cent
of the chain stores are located, you serve the customers,
mainly women, the way you would serve them in a drug-
store or a supermarket. You have new dynamics coming
into play, affecting what people buy and affecting publishers
who wish to satisfy the needs of these customers.

"I'm an advocate of the big book chains, because when
I was growing up you could walk into Scribner's bookstore,
on Fifth Avenue, and unless you were out of Harvard the

clerks looked down their noses at you. They were over-educated for what they were doing, and basically forced you out of an unwelcoming environment. Scribner's is still a wonderful bookstore and still has a wonderful clientele. But so many people were afraid to go into a bookstore then that you didn't have a growth of the book-buying populace. Even now, of the free countries in the world the United States has one of the lowest per-capita book readerships. I've been on brief trips to China and Russia, and book reading there is *ten* times what it is in the United States. There has been an élitism here about reading books. Up to now, only a certain class read books, and the book-distribution mechanism was for that class. Now, all of a sudden—boom! You are feeding books to people who formerly read nothing. Obviously, I like to see independent bookstores thrive, but I'm an advocate of what has come with the big chains, because if people read a *terrible* book, at least there's a book in the house, and a child might say, 'Hey!,' and maybe the parents will say, 'We'll put some more books in the house instead of watching some stupid thing on television.' People say you can't publish good books now, because you don't have the outlets for them. Well! It was in the past that outlets didn't exist. The fact is that good-quality books do get into the stores. They sell, and they sell better than they ever did. Books on history and politics, and biographies, for example, are selling at five times the rate they ever did before, and selling in the chains as well as the quality stores. There's a selective mechanism at work. Sometimes a publisher will publish a commercial book and that might be sold to Waldenbooks and some people might say that's bad. I say it's good—better that people read a commercial book than read nothing. It's a step up.''

About conglomerate mergers and acquisitions, Snyder said, ''The mergers originated with the publishers. It wasn't a question of the conglomerates' going after the publishers. The publishers went after the conglomerates.'' About the general quality of the books being published in an era of conglomerate ownership, Snyder said, "I've been around when we at Simon & Schuster were privately held, when we were publicly held, and when we were conglomerately held, and except in the areas of professional management and merchandising I've seen no change." He said that the fears of critics that the conglomerates might exercise censorship of books were groundless. He denied that the conglomerates exercised any censorship, or even cast any shadow of censorship, over the content of the books that their publishing divisions deal in.

If any group was dominating the publishing business, Snyder said, it was the agents and the authors they represented. "Remember, the great editors of the past read whole manuscripts. Now you've got to the point where, as a publisher, you'll get *twelve pages* from an author as an outline or a sample of his book. They might be the best twelve pages you've ever read, but if you dare say, 'Hey, why don't you at least expand this into sixty pages, or even give me a complete manuscript?'—which was what you could do twenty years ago—the author's agent is going to say, 'If you don't buy on the basis of what I'm letting you see, you're out of business.' And if you don't want to make a decision on the basis of the twelve pages, Random House is going to do it or Doubleday is going to do it. So the danger is that you pay for those twelve brilliant pages, and unfortunately the five hundred and eighty-two other pages turn out to be not so good, but you're obligated to publish the book. *That's* why a lot of bad, bad books are being published—not because the publishing houses are conglomerate-owned.''

Referring to criticism of the supposed influence of conglomerate ownership on the quality of contemporary literature, especially criticism offered in various interviews by Roger Straus, Snyder said, "I've debated Mr. Straus till I'm blue in the face, and we've tried here to figure out why Mr. Straus keeps talking this way. The only answer we've come up with is that he's making good hay out of this issue. The innocents that buy this stuff! 'See, I'm a publisher who's small and simple and easy to deal with, and I'm not a part of this whole conglomerate act in communications, and I don't pay advances of any consequence, because I'm intellectually pure!' And lots of authors say, 'Oh, we *definitely* want to be published by Farrar, Straus. Who wants to get into that colossus of a Random House or a Simon & Schuster, conglomerately owned!' And Mr. Straus uses that very effectively for his own gain. And Mr. Straus is starting to pick up an awful lot of authors who get low advances. And Mr. Straus does not like the fact that we at Simon & Schuster have an economic credibility above his, and had it even when we were independently owned—before we merged with Gulf & Western. That we generated far more cash and advertised many more books than he could. And he rants and raves. We've worked awfully hard to be bigger and, we think, better than Farrar, Straus. That doesn't mean we don't think Roger is a wonderful publisher. But if we had the same books he does, I think we'd sell more copies and have those authors more widely read than he does, and that's really what an author wants."

When I brought up the subject of the ever-rising prices being paid for best-sellers, Snyder declared that the bidding for subsidiary rights had "gone beyond economic reality." It should be borne in mind, he said, that when a paperback publishing house miscalculates and pays, say, a million dollars for reprint rights to a book that is really worth just half a million, there are going to be problems, because "there's no way to make money on that kind of book. It's economically unviable. That's the stupidity that's happening in this business. I see some people buying books like that all day long, and even if a miracle should occur, they're still going to lose money. And you can see this happening with book after book in paperback publishing.

"Another thing. We're unique in the hardcover publishing business in that we make a substantial amount of money on our hardcover operations well before any sales of paperback or other subsidiary rights whatsoever. And there's no great trick to it. I don't see why our competitors don't work that way. To us, our rights are bonus money. We make at least nine, ten per cent profit before *any* sales of rights. All this talk that paperback houses determine our hardcover editorial policy is just not true. And we pay our people the highest salaries in the industry. And we pay our authors—unfortunately or fortunately—the highest advances in the industry. What you have to do is to realize the full potential of each type of publishing. You try to minimize your mistakes and maximize your opportunities."

I raised the question of the damage to some authors—in particular, the so-called middle authors and beginning authors—by all the emphasis on big books in trade publishing. "Sure, somebody's getting hurt by all this," Snyder said. "The rich are getting richer and the poor are getting poorer. It used to be that if you were a young person and wanted to be a writer, you could go to a publisher and get enough of an advance to live adequately till your next book. That no longer happens. An eight- or ten-thousand-dollar paperback sale does not occur anymore—either you sell the damned thing for half a million or you get nothing. So you can't keep your young people alive. And what happens is our hardcover house can't justify a fifteen-thousand-dollar advance, because we're not going to get paperback money. We can say, 'This guy is pretty good, maybe he'll make a million dollars someday.' That's a pretty good risk ratio. But people turn around and say, 'Where *are* the young writers? What are they doing?' They're writing screenplays, because they can't make a living writing books. Because the other guys are making two million dollars on a book and it's a finite pot. If as an author you're making two million dollars on a paperback deal when the paperback house is going to earn back only half a million, the writeoffs have to be taken off someplace. And that's what has happened. We're doing it to ourselves, as publishers, and the authors are doing it to *them*selves. And it's all 'I've got mine back, and I'm not worried about you.' As for the younger authors, publishers still do support new talent—even though Roger Straus says he's the only one doing it. The difference is that nowadays it's becoming more a matter of support than a matter of good business. Now we *know* we're going to lose certain moneys by this kind of support. Whereas previously you could economically justify publishing the work of these people, you now have to economically justify your support essentially by future hopes, not on the basis of present business. So from a bottom-line point of view that hits you negatively.''

Turning again to the charges made by critics that conglomerate ownership of publishing houses tends to have an inhibiting effect on writing that is likely to be offensive to the conglomerates, Snyder said, ''I know what the truth is, whether I'm owned by Gulf & Western or not. I know that not one book we've put out has been tampered with as far as the content of the book is concerned. I know that we are totally independent. I know that the only reason I'd lose my job here could be that we'd done very badly. Well, that could happen whether we were privately owned or owned by a conglomerate. The charge always made is that the conglomerate is interested only in the bottom line. Are you going to tell me that Bennett Cerf wasn't interested in the bottom line? Do you think that Roger Straus's *bank* isn't interested in the bottom line? Well, Roger can say, 'Maybe

I happen to have inherited so much money that I don't have to worry about banks.' According to that theory, only rich people who inherited their money could be publishers—because that's the way they could be independent.''

Speaking of independent publishers, but finally getting off the subject of Roger Straus, Snyder said that smaller independent publishers who merged with larger companies did so for the sake of the economic advantages of operating more efficiently. ''If you're a small company, you're always into the banks, and paying thirteen or fourteen per cent for it,'' he said. ''It's very hard to stay alive in that business environment. And the bigger companies have the bigger sales forces, and so on—we can do it more efficiently and better. Yet in the early days of these acquisitions the conglomerates often saw good numbers that didn't work out. Take the CBS purchase of Holt, Rinehart & Winston. I don't think CBS can ever justify the price. CBS paid almost literally ten times what that company was worth.'' CBS paid around two hundred million for Holt. ''However, these conglomerates, including CBS, had highly inflated stocks—stocks selling at twenty-to-one, thirty-to-one price-to-earnings ratios. But in the case of CBS and Holt, the ratio should have been something like six to one. So CBS was giving away a lot of cheap stuff. That's what I think forced a lot of these mergers. People were giving away a lot of highly leveraged stock. Now it's different. Because of the economics offered by a large corporation and the difficulties of operating a small company in this very uncertain business environment, if I had a small company now and a big company came to me, I'd sell in five minutes. You see people doing that, and suddenly the man running that little two-, three-million-dollar company is worth ten times as much as the manager of the company that bought him. And it's better to have a corporation as a banker than a banker as a banker, because bankers are mercurial, and corporations are in business.''

CHAPTER 11

The Boston Resisters

Not all the experiences of book publishers with conglomerates are as happy as those that Richard Snyder indicates his company, Simon & Schuster, has enjoyed with Gulf & Western. Nor has the prospect of coming under the control of a conglomerate been at all welcome to various independent-minded publishers, especially when they have already decided that a merger with a big company would not be in their best interests. Such was the case of the venerable and independently owned Boston publishing house of Houghton Mifflin when, in the spring of 1978, it became known that Western Pacific Industries—a conglomerate that at the time owned, among other things, the Western Pacific Railroad—had been making unusually large purchases of Houghton Mifflin common stock and possibly intended to buy even more of it. These purchases led to widespread speculation in the publishing and financial worlds that Western Pacific might be planning a takeover attempt—an attempt that would certainly not be unusual in an age when the control of many formerly independent publishing houses has fallen more and more into the hands of vast conglomerates. Houghton Mifflin came into being in 1832, and authors associated with the house have included

Henry David Thoreau, Henry Wadsworth Longfellow, and Nathaniel Hawthorne. The people at Houghton Mifflin were disturbed by the idea of a takeover, and some of the chief officers of the company subsequently made their feelings known publicly. Several months before Western Pacific's stock purchases came to light, I had met with Harold T. Miller, who has been the president and chief executive officer of Houghton Mifflin since 1973, to ask him about the trend toward conglomerate ownership in publishing. Miller received me in his office—a room containing, among other pieces, a desk once owned by Hawthorne—at Houghton Mifflin's corporate headquarters, on the thirtieth floor at One Beacon Street. I found him to be a man of courteous, sober mien and rather careful speech.

Miller told me that textbooks for elementary and high schools accounted for about sixty-six per cent of Houghton Mifflin's annual business, with books for college use accounting for ten per cent, several subsidiaries for fourteen per cent, and trade books for the remaining ten. He said that Houghton Mifflin had become a publicly held company in 1967, that since then it had on several occasions been "asked to join forces with someone else," but that when the people running the company considered the pros and cons of the proposed mergers they had turned the offers down. "We've always asked the people who came to us how joining forces with a bigger company would make us a better publisher," he told me. "And we've never been satisfied with the answers. The arguments advanced never really seemed to us to be very good ones. It was as if those people felt, mostly, that we should merge because it seemed to be the thing to do. Generally, the arguments offered us were on the order of 'If you become part of us, you will have all the advantages of a large corporation—the greater resources, the greater management skills, and the like.' We were not impressed. Because if you look at how some of the major publishing companies acquired by communications or electronics conglomerates were doing as independents in, say, the early nineteen-sixties and how they're doing today, they're not such major companies now. Suppose you specialize in textbooks, and you agree to merge with a big electronics corporation. Well, the day you start as a subsidiary of one of these operations you're paying the overhead costs that are geared to the financial structure of the electronics industry rather than to that of the book industry. You're likely to find that your opportunity to invest in research and in new textbook programs is impaired, because the head of the acquiring corporation is looking at how he can put his investment dollars where they will bring the most return, and where they will bring the greatest return isn't going to be in some textbook operation. At one time, acquiring textbook publishers seemed to be the glamorous thing for big companies to do, but when things get a little tight for the acquirer where is the textbook publisher as a subsidiary? And, of course, the same question applies even more seriously to trade-book publishing. We have tried very hard at Houghton Mifflin to maintain our independence as a company, and the fact that we've survived is an indication of the view that many of our shareholders take of the value of our independence. There are still a few descendants of the Houghtons and Mifflins around as substantial stockholders, you know, and they have very strong feelings on this issue."

Miller told me that of Houghton Mifflin's stock nearly half was owned either by descendants of the founders or by present or former employees. "We've been very fortunate in having so many stockholders who feel there must be a place in our society for a publishing house committed to good, sound basic publishing," Miller said. "And the feeling of independence permeates our whole group—the stockholders, the editors, and the authors the editors deal with. It disturbs me to hear this talk about books' being the software of the movie business. We're delighted that some of our authors write books that sell to the movies, but I object to the idea that we're supposed to think of ourselves as a software house. At Houghton Mifflin, frankly, we'll go after the big book where financially we can do so. But we at least have a policy that we'll make an honest determination of how well such a book will really do. We set firm limits on what we're going to offer at auctions of big books. Maybe when you're independent and it's your own money you're gambling with you're more conservative with it. We don't want to lose ourselves in the pursuit of blockbusters. We still feel we have a commitment to enable promising young writers to get a start in fiction and nonfiction, and we even do a few books of poetry every year. We feel that if we're going to go on as serious publishers we have to help young fiction writers, and when we see talented young writers we try to keep publishing their books, even though that might not be really profitable before the writers can break through with substantial successes. We published five books by Paul Theroux, in whose future we had confidence, before he came along with *The Great Railway Bazaar,* his first big success.''

From what I could gather, Houghton Mifflin was then prospering as a company. In 1977, its sales reached a high in the company's history, amounting to a hundred and twenty-four million dollars—an increase of fourteen per cent over its sales for the previous year. The trade division contributed to this rise, with sales amounting to about twenty million dollars—an increase of forty-eight per cent over those for 1976. One of the trade division's big successes that year was J. R. R. Tolkien's *The Silmarillion,* which was published in September, went almost immediately to the head of the best-seller list, and stayed there until well into 1978. In the financial pages of the *Times* of

October 5, 1977, I had noticed that Houghton Mifflin's stock, which had been selling at 15¾ earlier in the year, had risen to 18⅞—an increase that I surmised might in part reflect the degree to which Wall Street was impressed by the ability of such an old Boston publisher to come up with best-sellers by writers of quality.

But there was another reason behind the increased demand for Houghton Mifflin stock on Wall Street. At the start of the winter of 1977-78, Miller and his fellow-directors at Houghton Mifflin began to notice what he later called "some transactions that were a little unusual" in the trading of Houghton Mifflin stock. On March 3, 1978, notification of a trade of a hundred and twenty-five thousand shares of Houghton Mifflin common stock went over the New York Stock Exchange wire—a transaction whose size the directors of Houghton Mifflin found distinctly disquieting. Then, on March 9th, a bombshell burst at Houghton Mifflin headquarters in the form of a statement filed with the Securities and Exchange Commission—a document known as a Schedule 13D statement, which, under the Securities Exchange Act of 1934, must be registered with the commission when five per cent or more of a publicly owned company's stock has been acquired by any one purchaser. The statement, which Western Pacific sent to the officers of Houghton Mifflin, revealed that between October 20, 1977, and March 3, 1978, Western Pacific Industries had bought two hundred and twenty-one thousand five hundred shares of Houghton Mifflin stock, for four million six hundred thousand dollars, "in furtherance of [Western Pacific's] program to diversify its sources of income." To Miller and his colleagues, the news looked like the beginning of an attempt by Western Pacific Industries to acquire a dominant position in the company's financial affairs, if not an outright takeover attempt. This suspicion was reinforced on April 19th, when Western Pacific Industries filed another statement with the

S.E.C., announcing that the number of Houghton Mifflin shares it had bought now totalled three hundred and twenty-seven thousand four hundred—more than ten per cent of all the shares of Houghton Mifflin stock—and giving notice that it might buy still more.

Aside from its purchases of Houghton Mifflin stock, Western Pacific had no connection with the publishing business, and it had no experience with it. Western Pacific was a holding company that owned principally, among its corporate assets, the Western Pacific Railroad Company. The chairman of the Board of Western Pacific Industries was Howard A. (Micky) Newman, who, shortly after the purchase of the Houghton Mifflin stock was announced, was described in an article in *Forbes* as "engaged in some very fancy financial maneuvering." Certainly some interesting things had been going on in the relationship between Western Pacific Industries and the Western Pacific Railroad. Between July of 1977 and March of 1978, when the Houghton Mifflin stock purchases became public knowledge, the Western Pacific Railroad—which during the previous five years had paid an annual average of eight hundred thousand dollars in dividends to Western Pacific Industries—had suddenly paid out four million four hundred thousand dollars in dividends to Western Pacific Industries. The situation was described in the *Forbes* article:

> The Western Pacific Railroad sold $20-million worth of bonds last June in a public offering underwritten by a Salomon Brothers-led syndicate. There was, however, nothing in the prospectus suggesting that the railroad the bondholders were investing in was about to be unloaded by its parent company. Nor did Newman tell the bondholders that the railroad assets that underlay the loan were worth about 11 cents on the dollar. Nor could the bondholders have been pleased when the parent company diluted their collateral by suddenly paying itself a much-fattened dividend out of surplus.

It was a mere three months after the bonds were sold that Newman announced his proposal to "sell" (i.e., virtually give) the railroad, along with its $100 million-plus in debt, to a new company formed by its employees. Three months after that the railroad was appraised for $14 million—a full $110 million below book value.

What's in it for Newman and WPI? Plenty. They wipe $100 million in debt off their balance sheet. Better yet, they generate for WPI tens of millions of dollars in ordinary losses for tax purposes. How can property sales generate ordinary losses? It's the way the laws are written: Losses incurred in the sale of property used in a business can offset ordinary income. Since the holding company is selling rail assets instead of the railroad's stock, it—not the railroad—gets to keep huge operating tax-loss carryforwards. Newman is already on the prowl for acquisitions whose earnings he can shelter.

The old Boston publishing company was, it seemed, one of those potential acquisitions encountered on Newman's prowl.

The news of the amount of stock that Western Pacific had amassed by the third week in April was received with real consternation at Houghton Mifflin headquarters, and when the Boston press began running news items about a possible attempt at a takeover, several prominent Houghton Mifflin authors also reacted with concern. On March 28th, a letter to Miller signed by five Houghton Mifflin authors— Archibald MacLeish, Arthur M. Schlesinger, Jr., John Kenneth Galbraith, Daniel Yergin, and Daniel Schorr—and subsequently made public declared, "We would be deeply concerned by any action that jeopardizes in any way the present character of the company or the present management and certainly any step which involves the passage of control, actual or potential, to an outside interest with no academic or literary experience or background and no community identification."

Archibald MacLeish went a step further. On April 8th, 1978, before an audience of publishers and authors at the New York Public Library, where he was awarded the National Medal for Literature and an accompanying prize of fifteen thousand dollars for his services to literature—a medal and a prize that had been endowed in 1964 by Thomas H. Guinzburg, publisher of the Viking Press, in memory of his father, the late Harold K. Guinzburg, who founded Viking in 1925—MacLeish said a few words about the role that conglomerates were assuming in the book business. After expressing high regard for Harold Guinzburg's contributions to literature as an independent publisher, MacLeish warned of the threat to literature posed by large corporations whose only interest in books was, he said, "the bottom line" on their financial balance sheets. As the *Times* reported the following day, MacLeish went on to say that he was referring to "the contemporary practice by which certain corporations, having no connection with literature, no knowledge of literature, no interest in it, have acquired publishing houses not to enter publishing but to diversify their investments." He then identified the "certain corporations" as conglomerates, which he described as "corporate carnivores conceived by a new breed of corporate manipulators." He said that a number of publishing houses in New York had been taken over, and that "the epidemic" was now reported to have reached Boston. Without mentioning Western Pacific Industries by name, MacLeish declared that Boston's oldest and most respected publisher— "Henry Thoreau's, no less"—was under increasing pressure from a West Coast conglomerate.

Galbraith, Schlesinger, MacLeish, and other Houghton Mifflin authors also sent a joint letter to Newman, questioning the aim of Western Pacific's purchases of so much Houghton Mifflin stock and implying that if Western Pacific did achieve substantial control over the publishing company's affairs they would reconsider using Houghton Mifflin as their publisher in the future. In addition, a number of Houghton Mifflin authors wrote to Newman individually on the matter. One of the most forceful representations came from Professor Mary P. Dolciani, of the Mathematics Learning Center, at Hunter College. Professor Dolciani is the author of widely used mathematics textbooks published by Houghton Mifflin. As quoted in the press, she wrote Newman, "I believe that a number of outstanding authors in the field of education first signed up with Houghton Mifflin as a result of takeovers of other firms with which they worked. For my part, I originally chose Houghton Mifflin and have elected to stay with them because of their dedication to publishing and also because of their independent status." And she strongly implied that if that status changed so might her interest in remaining a Houghton Mifflin author.

The chairman of Western Pacific reacted angrily to this uprising of authors. In an interview with Herbert Mitgang reported in the *Times,* Newman questioned the motivation of the authors' protests. "This whole thing sounds like a spontaneous demonstration in the Soviet Union," he declared. "I believe that the authors were put up to it by whoever is advising Houghton Mifflin. All the letters to me have the same tenor. It sounds like the party line."

To Professor Dolciani—again, as quoted in the press— Newman wrote that her letter had the flavor of having been written or suggested by "someone other than you." He told her, "You speak of Houghton Mifflin as having a 'dedication to publishing' as though that were a unique quality instead of a description of a publisher. What else do publishers do? Are you under the impression that Houghton Mifflin is not a profit-motivated business?" He went on:

Houghton Mifflin is only an entity created by law. The ultimate thrust of your letter is to gratuitously offer a warning or threat misdirected to Western Pacific because it has made an investment in a business enterprise for which you profess high regard. You know little or nothing about the persons of whom the management of Western Pacific is comprised, their philosophy of management, or their interests or aspirations.

When Mitgang asked the president of Houghton Mifflin about Newman's remarks and his reply to Professor Dolciani's letter, Miller said, "Can anyone honestly think that I could orchestrate Archibald MacLeish, or that I am capable of structuring John Kenneth Galbraith? . . . This attitude [of Newman's] shows the lack of understanding about the individuals in publishing and proves what the authors are saying in their letters."

On May 10th, the Authors Guild entered the fray. On behalf of the Guild, John Brooks, its president, Roger Angell, its vice-president, John Hersey, the chairman of its contracts committee, and Irwin Karp, its counsel, wrote a letter to Griffin B. Bell, then the Attorney General of the United States, and Michael Pertschuk, the chairman of the Federal Trade Commission, urging that the Justice Department or the F.T.C. "investigate the possibility that the Houghton Mifflin company may be acquired by Western Pacific Industries, Inc." They did so on the ground that "Western Pacific's acquisition of Houghton Mifflin would continue the trend to concentration that has destroyed the independence of many major publishing companies acquired by conglomerates and huge publishing complexes," and they declared that the acquisition of Houghton Mifflin by Western Pacific, if it occurred, could constitute a violation of the Clayton Anti-Trust Act, since it could lessen competition in the book-publishing industry—a situation that the signatories maintained would interfere with "the uninhibited marketplace of ideas protected by the First Amendment."

This move was a particularly powerful thrust against any possible takeover of Houghton Mifflin by Western Pacific, not only because the letter suggested that the Clayton Act might be applicable to this potential acquisition but also because the letter was bound to generate unfavorable publicity that might influence Western Pacific stockholders, and because the very existence of the letter raised the spectre of a whole variety of tiresome governmental inquiries into the financial affairs of the conglomerate. And, to stir up a bit further the literary hornet's nest that Western Pacific had stepped into, Miller and his co-directors of Houghton Mifflin had in the meantime decided to fight fire with fire, if necessary, by hiring the law firm of Skadden, Arps, Slate, Meagher & Flom to represent their interests. The people at Western Pacific may well have looked upon this as a serious matter, partly because the firm had gained wide experience in representing corporate raiders in takeover attempts as well as representing various potential corporate victims of such attempts, and knew a great deal about all the maneuverings in such corporate high-noon confrontations. What with the big public row raised by the well-known Houghton Mifflin authors—probably the first really effective collective action ever taken by authors of an independent publishing house facing a potential conglomerate takeover—and the forceful representations of the Authors Guild to the Justice Department and the F.T.C., and the knowledgeable legal counsel retained by Houghton Mifflin, Western Pacific must have given serious thought to whether it wanted to go through with further major acquisitions of Houghton Mifflin stock.

In fact, in the summer of 1978 Western Pacific in effect gave up the prospect of continuing its Houghton Mifflin stock purchases. In July, Houghton Mifflin entered into an agreement with Western Pacific to buy the three hundred and twenty-seven thousand four hundred shares of its common stock that Western Pacific held. After the agreement was announced, Newman was quoted in the *Times* as saying of the resistance by Houghton Mifflin and its authors and literary allies to Western Pacific's stock-purchasing program, "I really didn't expect the reaction we got there." However, his company did very well financially out of the affair. It had bought the stock at an average price of about twenty-one dollars a share. Now Houghton Mifflin paid thirty dollars a share for that stock, so within a few months Western Pacific had got something like a thirty-six-per-cent return on its investment. And Newman was quoted in the *Times* as saying that Western Pacific might set its sights on another publishing house. "There are all sorts of publishing companies, and I'm not going to ignore an opportunity that may come along because of what happened with Houghton Mifflin," he said.

A few months after Houghton Mifflin bought its stock back, I went to Boston and had a short talk with Austin Olney, vice-president in charge of the company's trade-book division. Olney made it clear that the reaction of everybody at Houghton Mifflin to the successful settlement with Western Pacific was one of enormous relief. He told me that Western Pacific's purchases of Houghton Mifflin stock had come as a complete surprise to people in the company, "even though we sensed that we were a ripe plum ready for the picking" by some acquisitive conglomerate. "I was excited by the way everyone closed ranks and got ready to fend off boarders," he said. He went on to say that the initial news that Western Pacific was moving in with substantial stock purchases had caused a moment of panic— "just trying to think of what to do"—within the company but that Harold Miller and his colleagues had quickly settled down to tackle the problem of takeover by getting sound legal advice. "We listened to everything the lawyers said, but I think the most pleasing thing that happened was when our authors got wind of what was going on and decided to help,'' he told me. ''In particular, Ken Galbraith, who after all is not without considerable background in the structure of large corporations, gave us some good advice, and in addition he acted on his own initiative to make various public comments on the situation. And in no time at all, without our ever having to go to our authors and say, 'Help save us,' they *were* helping, by the letters they sent expressing their serious concern about what was going on. We didn't say to them, 'Please do it—we'll go down the drain without your help.' To do that might have been of doubtful ethics. And it could be charged that we were not representing the best interests of the stockholders by trying to enrage our house authors against Western Pacific Industries. But we had other responsibilities, to both our authors and our stockholders. When our authors came forward with letters, we did circulate, with their permission, copies of them to other authors. And I think that a publishing house that didn't inform its authors of something like this situation would not be acting in good faith.''

After talking with Olney, I had another chat with Miller. He, too, was obviously pleased by the outcome of the Western Pacific crisis. ''I wouldn't like to go through anything like that again. It takes too much out of everybody,'' he said. I got some idea of Miller's feelings about takeovers when he passed on to me a few clippings from business magazines and financial newsletters, and some copies of speeches. One of the clippings was from a Wall Street newsletter, quoting from testimony by Robert J. Buckley, chairman and president of Allegheny Ludlum Industries, before the Antitrust, Monopoly, and Business Rights Subcommittee of the Senate Judiciary Committee:

> Call them ''takeovers,'' ''raids,'' or what have you . . . hostile mergers are not in the business interest, the customers'

interest and really not in the public interest, though they are often in the interest of the shareholders. Or at least the shareholders of a particular moment. . . .

A smaller, successful company that becomes healthy and liquid becomes a target of opportunity of some business that has not been managed well and needs the former's cash. This is plain old "blood-sucking," usually imparting only temporary life to the one and ending the existence of the other.

Also among the papers that Miller handed me was the transcript of a speech made by Richard E. Cheney, vice-chairman of the New York public-relations firm Hill & Knowlton, before the Business Roundtable and entitled "The Torrent of Takeovers—Is Any Relief in Sight for the Threatened Independent Executive?" In his speech, Cheney had referred to the successful resistance of the Houghton Mifflin management and its authors to the advances of Western Pacific, and he had commented, "So, it's still not impossible to ward off a takeover, given time and luck. But it continues to get more difficult, all the same." And, speaking of alleged economic benefits in growth, efficiency, and so on that are claimed to result from the takeover of smaller companies by large ones, Cheney asked:

Does growth by takeover really lead to economy of scale? This is a serious question. It has been pointed out that today it is not the backward unproductive company that is sought by raiders, but rather the more successful enterprise whose record of growth makes it an attractive target. If such a well-managed company is taken over, what happens to its effectiveness? Moreover, is there a tendency for the takeover company's planners to make planning decisions differently than the acquired company's planner might have. . . . In allowing takeovers to go unchecked, are we simply satisfying the egos of acquisitors or helping them get big enough to discourage takeovers by others and, if so, is that in the public interest?

To this Cheney added, "Admittedly I make my living in

part out of the takeover business, but I believe these questions should be examined by Congress."

Next, I looked at a photocopy of an article from *Business Week*. A few passages had been marked for Miller's attention. One dealt with Rudolph Eberstadt, the former president of Microdot—which he had helped to found and had headed for sixteen years—and his reaction after he resigned following the acquisition of Microdot by Northwest Industries. It read, "Although Eberstadt's reasons [for his resignation] were varied, when asked to sum them up in one sentence, he responds, 'I just wasn't used to having a boss.' " Another passage in the *Business Week* article read, "No matter how you cut it, superimposed authority is a bitter pill to swallow. Acquired managers' egos can be subjected to a constant and brutal battering. . . . And they are expected to change their perspective on decisions almost overnight: What works for their operation as a company may not work for it as a division."

For all that, Miller, though he was only too glad to have the Western Pacific affair behind him, seemed rather uncomfortable about what people might expect of him as president of Houghton Mifflin, in view of his ordeal. "I want to be honest about our relations with our authors and what they did concerning Western Pacific's purchase of stock," he told me. "To say that we had no conversations with the authors about our position would be to misrepresent the situation. They always knew where I stood. But what they did developed on its own, and beyond any capacity we might have for controlling them, even if we wished to. No publisher can put his authors in lockstep. I have a stack of letters from authors who are not our own authors and from people who work at other publishing houses expressing their pleasure at our stand on resisting this thing, and about the way it all turned out. I'm very appreciative of what our authors did, but I don't want to dwell on it. I don't want to appear to be using them. And I don't want to be the darling of the authors' group that protested, or of the Authors Guild. And I don't want to be placed in the camp that says there's no good purpose in a merger, because there can be a point where for good and proper reasons a publishing entity might wish to seek association with other publishers, say.''

CHAPTER 12

"An Inspired Merger"

W<small>HEN</small> Archibald MacLeish delivered his public denunciation of conglomerates' acquisitions of publishing houses, what he had to say must have been received with a certain bemusement by Thomas Guinzburg, of Viking. Guinzburg assumed the presidency of Viking in 1961, after the death of his father. In 1975, Guinzburg and his sister, Carola Lauro, sold two-thirds of their virtually total financial control of Viking to Penguin Books, the American subsidiary of the big British paperback house, for a price that has been estimated at nine million dollars. Under the terms of the merger, Guinzburg became the president and chief executive officer of a new company, Viking Penguin, Inc., and also continued to direct Viking's editorial affairs. The merger of such a widely respected American hardcover publishing house—which in its fifty-year history had published a distinguished list of fiction and nonfiction works, including books by James Joyce, Dorothy Parker, D. H. Lawrence, John Steinbeck, Rebecca West, Stefan Zweig, and Saul Bellow—and the major British publisher of quality paperback books seemed to give great satisfaction to both parties. In an article in the *Times*, Alden Whitman reported, "Mr. Guinzburg, for his part, bubbled with optimism over

Viking Penguin, Inc. 'I expect to improve and strengthen the present Viking list,' he said, 'by attracting authors who can be published in either trade or paperback. . . . In my view, publishing as a whole will gain from this merger.' "
By the spring of 1978, however, Guinzburg was having his troubles with the parent company. These troubles climaxed in September of 1978, when the new owners removed Guinzburg from the presidency of Viking Penguin. He was replaced by Irving Goodman, who had been the publisher of trade books at Holt, Rinehart & Winston.

In the spring of 1979, I had a chance to talk to Guinzburg at his apartment, in New York, about his experiences at Viking and about what had happened after his company was taken over by Penguin—a version of events that may differ, of course, from that of the new owners but that does nonetheless provide an example of the difficulties an independent publisher may have to contend with in a merger with a conglomerate. Penguin Books are produced by the Penguin Publishing Company, which was started by Allen (later Sir Allen) Lane in 1935, and the books were originally so inexpensive that they were sold in Britain through Woolworth's. Sir Allen Lane died in 1970, and almost immediately thereafter the company was acquired by Longman, Ltd., the English publishing company. Longman is part of the Pearson-Longman group, which is a holding company controlling the varied publishing activities of S. Pearson & Son, a conglomerate with extensive interests—oil and manufacturing interests among them—in Britain, Europe, and the United States.

Guinzburg began his talk with me by saying that most people, and even people in the business itself, didn't really appreciate the enormous changes that had occurred in publishing since the nineteen-twenties. "Knopf had started earlier, but Viking, Random House, and Simon & Schuster all started up between 1924 and 1927, and very few people realize how small these companies were," he said. "It was a cottage industry they went into. They were started mostly by very young people, like my father—young people whose families were well-to-do. Most of these people were there to represent quality rather than popular literature. There weren't a great many bookstores in the country then, and there were no bookstore chains. In addition to starting Viking Press, my father started the Literary Guild, and the reason he did so was that there were so few bookstores in the country and so many people seemed embarrassed about going into the bookstores that did exist. The book clubs made the process of picking out readable books much easier for such people. At Viking, the change from cottage industry to the semi-big time occurred in the late nineteen-fifties and early sixties. Then came the big time in TV, the rise of the big electronics companies, and the whole Jules Verne promise of electronic miracles ahead. We all read reports about that and shook in our boots: if you listened to the doomsday spokesmen of that period, TV was going to put the traditional publishers out of business. Well, we know what came of most of those promises about the electronic classroom and all that. But the book-publishing business seems to be following the TV pattern, in some ways. Just like TV, the book business has been affected by a jackpot syndrome. You have a *Holocaust,* which was created for TV before it was a book. Increasingly, the distribution of books is in the hands of a few people, just as TV is, and the battle to get on the racks through the distributors isn't much different from the battle among the TV networks to hang on to their affiliated stations.

"All right. When it comes to the considerations lying behind the Viking merger with Penguin, you have to recognize that, generally, when the big electronics-industry push of the sixties came along, independent publishing companies like Viking Press were significantly undercapitalized, and when the acquisition by the big communications companies of houses like Random House occurred, in the sixties and seventies, and at the same time you had an enormous growth of the mass-market paperback and a scramble for blockbuster books, houses like Viking found themselves under pressure to keep up in the marketplace. Having been a very good small publishing house for so long, Viking had begun to be a very good medium-sized publishing house. Having been essentially a literary publisher, we had begun to find the occasional commercial *and* good book. We had Saul Bellow, who hadn't been very successful at first, and who began to be very successful. And I remember one glorious day in 1970 when four of the ten best-selling books were by our authors, including Bellow and Graham Greene. As we had more than our normal share of success, and the writers we had or wanted needed greater financial backing for future books and acquired agents who could command far bigger advances than formerly, we had to consider how we were going to be able to supply all this vastly increased financing. The price of the success that Viking was enjoying—whether in the cost of maintaining our authors, with large advances against future royalties, or of doing business generally—had come to exceed our flow of cash. Cash flow is the Catch-22 of the publishing business, because the business has been so undercapitalized. Let me give you just one example, concerning a commercially successful writer, of the kind of rise in cash advances that were required. When Frederick Forsyth's book *The Day of the Jackal* was published, in 1971, he got about a ten-thousand-dollar advance. For his second Viking book, *The Odessa File,* he got a half-million-dollar advance, and for his most recent book, *The Devil's Alternative,* he got an advance not far from two million dollars. Soon, with the huge escalation in advances being demanded by writers and their agents, we found we had reached the point where we could not conduct business in terms of available cash, and we realized that we'd have to go to the banks and tell them we'd need so many dollars, and we had to face the fact that they just might say that a loan to us would not be a good business risk—or, alternatively, they might take an equity position in our business as a condition for the loan.

"So at that point we said we guessed we needed some partners, and we began to look around for some. We had a lot of suitors, and most of those that we entertained seriously were already involved in publishing. One of them was Penguin Books. We didn't have a major paperback arm of our own, and in the past Penguin had tried on three different occasions to create an increased position with us but hadn't succeeded, so there were honest brokers out there still trying to arrange a marriage between Penguin and Viking. I went to see Felix Rohatyn, of [the investment-banking house of] Lazard Frères. Felix told me that Lazard could be of assistance to us in arranging a merger with Penguin on terms agreeable to us. Everything looked all right to us, and we thought we should go ahead and merge with Penguin Books. In fact, we thought at the time that it would be an inspired merger—a quality American hardcover house joining forces with what is, outside the United States, the foremost quality paperback house in the English-speaking world. And we knew, of course, that behind Penguin lay the extremely impressive assets of the Pearson group, and its ownership of newspapers and periodicals, including the *Financial Times* of London, and its part ownership of *The Economist*. It owns a bit of Ashland Oil, it owns a lot of land in California. It has extensive interests in Africa. It owns Royal Doulton china; it owns the Château Latour vineyards—one of the great inducements! No matter how we looked at it—on top, underneath, and all around— the arrangement looked very good. And to us one of the biggest attractions of a merger with Penguin was that it was *over there*—it would be less likely to be looking over our shoulder all the time than any domestic conglomerate setup. There wouldn't be that sense of control right on our doorstep. I remember Bennett Cerf once talking about what is involved in an acquisition of a publishing house by a big company—in the case of Random House, of course, by RCA. Bennett said, 'I hope you never have to do it. It becomes more difficult every week.'

"Well, we went ahead with the merger with Penguin. What was involved was more a transfer of financial control than a merger, but my capacity for maintaining working control over Viking's affairs seemed extraordinarily secure. In working out the arrangements, the people who acted for me and my family were successful in writing a contract concerning my own role which was unlike most contracts for chief executives in merger situations, where you can continue to run your own company but don't have any legislative teeth. My piece of paper said I had complete control and would continue to run Viking without any outside interference. And so the merger went through.

"And there we were, all very happy. The merger of Viking and Penguin—it's a tale called 'Welcome to the Conglomerate.' And the red carpet that was put out for us when this fascinating arrangement was completed was quite genuine. At Viking, we felt we'd created the best possible circumstances for continuing our professional lives, and for the ultimate benefit of all the writers we would be publishing. Through Penguin, because it's such a strong house, we could see our writers being distributed in places where they had never dreamed of having their books sold—for example, in Singapore, in the Far East generally, in Australia, in Nigeria. It seemed like an enormously attractive arrangement in this respect, and I think it still is. And, in addition, the distribution of Penguin Books in the United States has taken very significant steps forward since the arrangement between the two houses was consummated.

"But what was not successful, I found, was our ability to mesh two different styles of publishing and of management. I found that the English management, which was the dominant one, operated primarily through committee and was heavily freighted with computerization and meticulous financial forecasting—all of which was set directly against the smaller, personal, idiosyncratic style here. As an independent publishing house, Viking had never been run as a democracy, you know; it was run as a sort of benevolent dictatorship, I suppose, but it was one in which our *instinct* for books was always central. After this merger took place, we never really comprehended or were able to absorb the fact that, for example, there was a gigantic computer in our midst—a computer hooked up to a terminal in Baltimore that was supposed to tell us, on the basis of all the known factors at a particular time for decision, what the price of every Viking book should be. If we were to accept the analysis offered by that computer, certainly every book that we put out under the new scheme of things at Viking could be published profitably. The only catch was that the books would have to be priced so high that nobody could afford to read them. You can't legislate publishing decisions by big-company computer. What we were used to had to do with publishers' smell—with what we felt *comfortable* publishing. I found that our own decisions were more and more being dictated from thirty-five hundred miles away and by the sort of computer-oriented thinking I've mentioned. That's just one symptom of what I felt was beginning to do us in. To be truthful, the qualitative problems we had with the Penguin complex in England were real ones. Fine as Penguin is, it's essentially a paperback house, which does comparatively little original publishing. It had no interest in hardcover publishing, even though it owned its own hardcover house in London—Allen Lane, which was a sort of feeding station for Penguin reprints. And, irrespective of the fanfare with which the merger with Viking had been greeted in Britain, I could not believe that there was any significant support for a hardcover publishing program in which Viking would have a prominent place. It was made absolutely, explicitly clear to us that the weight of investment dollars was going to stay significantly on the Penguin side. And Viking, it was hoped in Britain, would act primarily as a producer of books whose ultimate sale would be in Penguin. In other words, Viking would become another feeding station for Penguin.''

Interestingly, in view of the assumption by a number of critics of the conglomerate role in book publishing that conglomerate-owned publishers, when they embark on a policy of big advances and big books, are having to do so as a result of direct orders from conglomerate headquarters, Guinzburg made it clear to me that what he described as "one of the areas where we had the most fundamental disagreement" was "the degree to which Viking, in hardcover, should remain competitive on the successful-author level." Which is to say that in this situation it was not Viking's corporate owners but Guinzburg himself who was all for Viking's being in the big-money, big-book publishing race as well as in the business of publishing books of literary quality. Guinzburg's explanation of this rather curious state of affairs—which seemed to me to offer an example of the conflicts not only between a formerly independent publisher and his conglomerate owners but also between the entrepreneur and the littérateur in Guinzburg himself—was this: "It remains my conviction that the book for which one is most likely, as a publisher, to pay the most money is a book that is likely to start immediately generating a return on that money. If you pay a vast amount of money for a writer's work, the amount is usually based on some sort of track record. As soon as one commits oneself to one of these hefty advances, the entire publishing community begins to respond. The Book-of-the-Month Club or the Literary Guild may make some kind of commitment simply on the basis of the news of the size of the advance, merely to get an option on the book, and this, in turn, generates monetary enthusiasm from other parts of the industry—mass-market paperbacks, magazines, foreign publishers. I'd rather make one of these big advances to some author in whom I have confidence than make ten smaller advances to those in whom I have less confidence—those books may never be written. A person you give a five-thousand-dollar advance to is less likely to produce—it's not the greatest priority in his life. 'Unpublished advances'—that's our R. & D. You must spend a lot of money this way, but you can't get careless about it. What used to be a three-thousand-dollar advance to a young author is now a ten-thousand-dollar advance, and one of your painful tasks at the end of the year is to look over your list and write off those books that their authors are never going to finish.''

Guinzburg went on, ''And there were other disagreements over our degree of access to all the formidable assets of the Pearson group, which had so attracted us in the first place. At one stage, I went to London about getting additional financing that I had asked for and that I believed we needed at Viking. Later on, Lord Gibson, the chairman of S. Pearson & Son, made a trip to New York, and after seeing the Viking operation he said to me that, while he understood our request for more money, 'I have to decide whether to give it to you or to put it into pistachio nuts.' Well, that about summed it up for me. The words can't be avoided, there's no use pussyfooting around it: this is what was being emphasized to the American subsidiary—'profitability,' 'net profit,' 'bottom line,' or just 'the line.' Oh, how that grates on my brainpan! That's something you used to hear in the garment industry. But not about the books of individual authors. I spent three years in that merger with our British colleagues, and there was a lot of piety about what we were publishing, but actually the only real interest was in how we were going to do this year, and the next year, and the next year again. One was just constantly engaged in the kind of financial projections that anyone in financial management might be used to—but a publisher concerned primarily with the literary quality of the books he handles isn't, necessarily. It seemed that we spent most of the year preparing financial projections for next year for Penguin, and, on top of that, three-year projections. 'What are you going to do to increase your profitability?' This was the incessant question when they saw our statements.

" 'Well,' it was suggested, 'you can cut down on your overhead.' That's usually the first emergency surgery that takes place. Attrition of staff people. Cut down on the copyediting staff—during the recession of 1977, the copyediting departments of trade-book publishing were probably cut down more than any other departments. Cut down on advertising: that's very significant, because by cutting down in small increments on advertising expenditures you can seem to save huge sums; a couple of percentage points off your advertising-and-promotion budget could go into hundreds of thousands, and since advertising is a straight out-of-pocket expense, your savings are visible immediately. And, of course, raise the price of your books. You can do all these things in response to pressures. But the pressures don't stop when you do respond that way. Pretty soon, you start concentrating your attention on publishing books you *know* will be successful. Instead of really putting yourself behind people who might be fine writers but not writers to support really profitably, you begin to go after several of a hundred successful names. That's what can happen to a publisher under pressure, and if the publisher is saying that to himself you can be sure he's saying it to his editorial staff. And the editors begin to respond to that pressure. They even find the character of their lunches changing; instead of talking over the structural problems of an author's book, they're making *contracts* at lunch. And telling themselves, 'Well, maybe I won't send up that proposal for that first novel after all—maybe I can find a sexy thriller.'

"Things just began to go bad. And one of the reasons they went bad, and from bad to worse, was the attention I was drawing to myself by becoming increasingly outspoken about the degree of stress and pressure the Penguin management was creating, and by making it clear I didn't believe that the people I was dealing with on the other side of the Atlantic were as competent to make American publishing decisions as we were here at Viking. And I guess that I was outspoken about what became a disdain for their failure to understand our publishing philosophy or our particular problems. Word of this was certainly conveyed to the English proprietors, who ultimately began to see me as a disgruntled and less than faithful follower of an over-all corporate plan, and someone who was unchangeably convinced of the soundness of his own publishing philosophy. The people at Penguin weren't colleagues anymore. They were the owners—the proprietors. They had financial control over Viking. They owned two-thirds of the stock, my family owned one-third. I had that wonderful contract, it was true, giving me full decision-making powers at Viking. They could not impose control over my decision-making powers while I was on the scene. However, a contract is really not a guarantee of anything except that you'll be paid. The proprietors couldn't break my contract, but I was breakable."

From *Publishers Weekly*, October 2, 1978:

In these developments that spanned the Atlantic: Peter Mayer [former president and publisher of Pocket Books] was appointed chief executive officer of Penguin International, which comprises independent publishing operations worldwide, including Viking Penguin Inc. in the U.S.; and Thomas H. Guinzburg was succeeded as president and chief executive officer of Viking Penguin Inc. by Irving Goodman, publisher of trade books at Holt, Rinehart, and Winston for the past four years.

The announcements of the two new appointments were made September 26 by E. J. B. Rose, chairman and chief executive of the Penguin Publishing Company.

Considering Guinzburg's original intent in selling control of Viking to Penguin and the Pearson interests—that is, to have access to the strong financial resources of an international conglomerate in order to assure stability and expansion of his book company's operations—it seems ironic that only five years after the merger Viking's controlling company, Penguin, rather than Viking itself, displayed signs of serious problems. In February of 1980, Penguin Books, Ltd., announced that it was cutting its publishing program by some twenty-two per cent, dismissing a hundred people out of a total of six hundred on its staff, and lowering its overhead drastically. These measures included reducing the number of new books being published from five hundred and twenty-five to four hundred and seven. Furthermore, the number of Penguin books in the company's warehouses was to be reduced by four million. Peter Mayer, when he took over at Penguin at the time of Guinzburg's departure from Viking, had embarked on a program of acquiring popular works for the Penguin series, dropping those titles that, he later said, were "going to too small a market," and buying what he called "more accessible" works, which were promoted and marketed aggressively, more or less in the American paperback-publishing manner. "Good backlist titles are being dropped to pay for best-sellers," one Penguin staff member said in a story in the *Times*. Quite apart from these considerations, however, Penguin's dependence on the overseas market, including the American (forty per cent of its business has been overseas), combined with the growing weakness of the dollar against the British pound and the extraordinarily high British inflation and interest rates, has been responsible for hurting Penguin's business badly, as it has hurt the British book business in general. When Mayer had been in the American mass-market-paperback-publishing business, first at Avon and then at Pocket Books, his colleagues considered him to be one of the more capable and energetic publishers on the scene, and it may be that at Penguin he was confronted with economic conditions essentially beyond his control. In any event, a publishing company with an honorable history—the company that Guinzburg had once looked to with such hope as Viking's bulwark of protection and aid—found itself struggling to stay afloat.

William Targ, a vigorous and sportily dressed man of seventy-three, regularly enjoys a comfortable prospect as he presides over lunch at a corner table in the main dining room of the Algonquin. There he daily entertains friends and acquaintances, including many figures in the publishing business, among whom he is well known as a veteran editor and a genial host. Targ began to make a name for himself in the publishing business in the nineteen-forties, when he developed the trade-book division of World Publishing. In 1963, World was bought by the Times Mirror Company, of Los Angeles, which had entered the paperback-book business three years previously by acquiring New American Library. At the time of the Times Mirror acquisition, Targ was a vice-president of World and a member of its board of directors. "The Times Mirror representatives told us they were there to help us grow," Targ said later on. "I had spent twenty-one years in developing the trade-book division from scratch, and two weeks after the Times Mirror people took over we were told that all contracts for hardcover trade books made by World had to be approved by the New American Library paperback people." Targ decided to leave this conglomerate setup, and joined the independent publishing house of G. P. Putnam's Sons as a senior editor. Putnam, a widely respected hardcover house, had been founded by George Palmer Putnam in 1838 (just six years after Houghton Mifflin was established as a publishing company) and had been the publisher of such authors as Edgar Allan Poe and Washington Irving. In 1932, control of G. P. Putnam's Sons had been acquired by Melville Minton, a former salesman for Charles Scribner's Sons, who became president of Putnam and ran it until his death, in 1955. He had been succeeded as president by his son Walter J. Minton, and it was under Walter Minton's presidency that Targ joined Putnam and, later, became the company's editor-in-chief. In that role, Targ, over the years, acquired a number of works that turned out to be huge commercial successes, most notably *The Godfather*, which he bought from Mario Puzo for an advance of five thousand dollars in 1967, whereupon Putnam sold the paperback rights to it to Fawcett for four hundred and ten thousand dollars. As editor-in-chief at Putnam, Targ was also responsible for the company's publishing a large number of other authors, ranging from Simone de Beauvoir to Art Buchwald. A man who vastly enjoyed the life of an independent editor, Targ was disappointed to learn, in 1975, that the status of Putnam as an independent house was about to change. That year, Minton decided to sell control of Putnam to MCA, the entertainment and so-called leisure-time conglomerate. Under the terms of sale, Minton remained as president.

Over a Gibson at his table at the Algonquin—a drink that he said the editor Maxwell Perkins had introduced him to years ago—Targ reminisced about his experiences at Putnam after MCA acquired control. "Walter Minton sold Putnam to MCA because he thought it advantageous for his family to own MCA stock," Targ told me. "Mr. Minton certainly didn't sell the company because Putnam was short of cash. Putnam had never borrowed from a bank. In fact, Putnam *lent* money to banks. It had an eight-million-dollar cash reserve when it sold to MCA. In my view, even at the time, there was no logical reason having to do with publishing itself for selling the business. I said to Walter Minton before the deal went through, 'If you sell Putnam to MCA, six months later you're going to be fired.' He said to me, 'I can't be fired. I have a *contract.*' So MCA acquired us. They told us, 'We're here to help you.' But as far as I was concerned we didn't need any help."

After MCA bought Putnam, Targ said, "our editorial meetings suddenly began to feel the impact of the mother company." He continued, "This impact deepened as time went on. I remember one editorial meeting in 1978 when Mr. Minton told us, 'The emphasis will be on entertainment.' That's verbatim. I said, 'All fiction is entertainment.' Minton said, 'We want to do more tie-ins with films, television shows, and there are a lot of novelization possibilities.' I had brought a lot of commercially successful books to Putnam, but I also wanted to find new writers. I was publishing some interesting new writers, and I wanted to seek out more of them. But I discovered, for the first time in my publishing career—and in spite of the fact that I was, after all, editor-in-chief of Putnam—that there was to be no chance for these people at Putnam unless there was a substantial sale of subsidiary rights to their work *up front.* I went to the advertising department to discuss advertising for the book of a new writer. I was told, 'Wait a minute.

There's no budget for that book.' We had a meeting about it. At it, I was told again, 'There's no budget for that—not one dime for advertising that book, because no subsidiary rights to it have been sold.' I went to Peter Israel, Putnam's managing director, about the matter. He said to me, 'What's the use of throwing money away on books that can't make it?' I said, 'I'm old-fashioned, I guess, but what's the use of this business if you can't take a *chance* on a book?' At another editorial meeting, I made a David-and-Goliath thing out of this issue. There were some young editors at Putnam who were proposing some authors they thought we ought to publish. I said at the meeting, 'Unless we agree to support young writers with advertising, I don't think we should be buying their work—because it's unfair, and because it's so embarrassing to work with an author for so many months and to know that after all that work that author is just not going to be supported by the publisher.' And I said to Peter Israel, 'Look, among all the books I bought for Putnam, those two Puzo books netted Putnam two and a half million dollars in paperback-rights income. Can't we peel off twenty thousand, thirty thousand dollars from this roll and put it into these new authors?' He said, 'No. That's not the way we work.' I wrote out my resignation, and said I would leave Putnam at the end of the year. One day when I was still there—early in December of 1978, I think—Walter Minton walked into my office and said, 'You won't believe this. I'm fired.' ''

CHAPTER 13

A Bidding Stratosphere

To TURN to less sombre—even strictly up-beat—aspects of the contemporary publishing scene, it proved to be a lucky day for Morton Janklow, the lawyer-agent, when, in March of 1976, he received in the mail for his consideration, from a friend in Beverly Hills, Mrs. Judith Krantz, the manuscript of a novel she had written. It was Mrs. Krantz's first effort at a novel, and she wanted Janklow's opinion of it. Mrs. Krantz, the wife of the movie producer Steven Krantz, had a background as a free-lance magazine writer on nonfiction subjects for such magazines as *Good Housekeeping, McCall's, Ladies' Home Journal,* and *Cosmopolitan.* Janklow is a busy man, and the manuscript was nine hundred and fifty pages long, but he took it home with him and read it anyway. What happened after he did so has been summed up by Mrs. Krantz this way: "Morty didn't get the manuscript till Friday. He called me on Monday, and he said to me, 'If you want to see that book covering the face of every woman on the beach in America next summer, let me be your agent.' "

The novel was about business, success, and sex on Rodeo Drive, the super-boutique row in Beverly Hills, and also about the movie business, and it was called *Scruples,* after the fictional name of a boutique founded by the central character. According to Mrs. Krantz, Janklow's first move after he took her manuscript on professionally was to show it to the people at Simon & Schuster; they turned it down, she said, "because they didn't like it," whereupon Janklow showed it to Larry Freundlich, then in charge of fiction at Crown Publishers, an independent hardcover house. (Freundlich is now an editor at Simon & Schuster.) Freundlich loved the manuscript, Mrs. Krantz said, and after several weeks of bargaining between Crown and Janklow "Crown bought my manuscript for a fifty-thousand-dollar advance, which was enormous for a first novel, and the next thing I knew Warner Books was shown the manuscript and they offered a preëmptive bid on the paperback rights of half a million dollars." She added, "I was reeling!"

Scruples was published by Crown, in a first printing of a hundred and six thousand copies, in March of 1978, and it went almost immediately to the top of the Times best-seller list. It stayed on the best-seller list for about a year. (So far, the hardcover edition has sold over a million copies in the United States and Canada.) The jacket of the book was distinguished by a color picture of the head of a fashionable-looking woman, in a close-fitting hat and a veil. One of Janklow's associates remarked later of Crown's merchandising of the book, "Scruples was completely packaged and jacketed to make it look very classy, which is one of the factors in this kind of image-making. A lot of the readers of such books as Scruples are middle-class and upper-middle-class housewives. If you were to say to them about one of these books, 'Do we have a dirty sex book for you!,' you might have a problem. In the packaging of Scruples everything was done to upgrade the image of the book and make it classy. Just as everything in the promotional tours that Judy Krantz made for the book was done first class."

In Mrs. Krantz, the people at Crown found, they had not

only a successful writer of popular fiction but also a publicizer of her own work whose determination and untiring energy were almost comparable to those of the late Jacqueline Susann. Mrs. Krantz crisscrossed the country making network and local TV and radio appearances to plug *Scruples,* and also put in appearances at supermarkets, shopping centers, bookstores, and women's-club meetings—any place where her book could be touted effectively. And when Warner issued *Scruples* in paperback, in the spring of 1979, she went on tour across the country all over again. I got my first glimpse of Judith Krantz in person at the 1979 convention of the American Booksellers Association, in Los Angeles, where for two hours she sat or stood autographing copies of the paperback edition of *Scruples* for attending booksellers, at the rate of about five hundred books an hour. "The local bookseller is so essential," Mrs. Krantz told me later. "These are key, key people. In their town, people call them up and say, 'What do you advise for Great-Aunt Minnie in the hospital?' They have lists of ladies who read. What they call 'clienteles.' People who call up and say, 'Sarah, what's new?' Near the Warner Books booth at the A.B.A. convention when I was autographing I looked at the name tags on the people lined up, to see if the tags had a blue border. That meant a bookseller. You don't want exhibitors who aren't booksellers picking up your book." Janklow was at the booksellers' convention, too—all over the place and terribly busy on the deal-or-chestration front, but also continually in touch with Mrs. Krantz. One day of the convention was proclaimed Judith Krantz Day by the mayor of Beverly Hills, in honor of the novelist's success with *Scruples.* At a party given by Warner Books at the Beverly Hills Hotel for her and A.B.A. people, Mrs. Krantz was in the reception line. Again, Janklow was on hand. "This is a meat-and-potatoes party," Janklow told me. He explained, "Look at all those other authors, out tonight at those flash agents' parties up on Mulholland Drive. *This* is meat and potatoes—the place is full of jobbers and regional and local distributors, and, as you can see, Judy is right in there, standing by the door shaking hands, talking to the wives, and remembering the names.''

While I was in the Los Angeles area, I had a talk with Mrs. Krantz at her home—a big, very comfortable house whose architectural style she has described as "California French provincial, I guess." Mrs. Krantz is a rather short, very perky-looking woman with blondish hair composed in a sort of upswept, what-are-the-wild-waves-saying style. She was wearing a blue turtleneck and light-salmon-colored pants. She had just returned from six weeks of cross-country TV, radio, and other appearances following the paperback publication of *Scruples,* she told me, and still more tours were ahead. "I never realized before how much hustling was involved," she said. "Touring for a book—it's the literary equivalent of war. I remember my hardcover tour. I'd hit a city—say, Cleveland—at night, unpack, steam out the clothes that were wrinkled, and, the next morning, get up at six. Because there's always an 'A.M. Show,' a 'Good Morning Show,' a 'Hello Show' in every city in the country. I happen to be naturally very hyper and jazzed up, so I never had to be actually awakened by a wake-up call. Also, I have a compulsive streak about being on time. When the wake-up call comes, I'll already be putting on my mascara. Men authors on tour can wake up, shave, and get right out of their hotels to go on television. A woman author can't. She has to put on all the makeup and do her hair. I had to learn to make myself up for television, because I have a rather allergic skin, and I have a tendency to break out when they make me up at the studio. Anyway, at most out-of-town stations they don't make people up, and when they do, the brushes and the powder puffs look as though they'd been used on twenty-five thousand people. So I make myself up. When you leave that hotel early in the morning, you have to be packed up and all checked out—the publisher has a limo to get you to the studio, and your suitcase is going to be in that limo all day while you make your sixteen different stops. Your arrival at the studio is at seven-thirty or eight, and the author invariably goes on last, but you have to be there an hour ahead of time in order to keep them from going crazy. Then, after I went on, I'd do a whole day of media in Cleveland, finishing up at six o'clock, just in time to catch a plane for Detroit, and the departure gate is *always* at the very end of the airport. You do that day after day and enough weeks in a row, and you get so that you feel you can hardly function. One day during the hardcover tour, after doing all those media appearances in St. Louis—on sheer adrenaline, I guess—suddenly I felt I'd had it. I felt they had used up every last ounce of my blood. My husband insisted I come back home to rest, and I came here and slept for about three days. Then I talked to Jim Zeidman, who was with the Doubleday Book Shop in Beverly Hills. I told him I'd used my last ounce of blood. He said, 'You get back out on that road. Irving Wallace does it. Sidney Sheldon does it. You do it. If you want your book to sell, you finish up that tour!' So I called Crown and said, 'Rebook it.' But the next time around, for the paperback tour, I laid down conditions with Warner. Only one city in a day, and no night travel, so I wouldn't arrive in the next city in a state of exhaustion.

"When I go on tour, I prepare ahead of time. I interview myself and prepare typical questions and answers for shows that I'm going to appear on. I tape these interviews with myself, and the Q-and-A's go out to every show ahead of time. And I see to it that these really *are* sent, along with the bios and all the other information. Before the hardcover tour for *Scruples,* Crown put out the best press kit ever invented, and two thousand went out to the press, TV, and radio, and to booksellers, too. Radio is very important in selling books, so I go on radio interview shows a lot. One thing about radio interviews—the station breaks come so often that the interviewers will keep saying after the breaks, 'We've been talking to Judith Krantz, the author of *Scruples,* the new best-seller.' On TV, all they do is flash that book for a few seconds. On all these shows, you don't talk about the plot of your book. You talk about Rodeo Drive. If I hadn't by good luck written about Rodeo Drive—which was just becoming the greatest shopping street of the Western world—when I did, I don't know how I could have got on 'The Merv Griffin Show' or 'The Mike Douglas Show.' And I think I've been on every local TV show that has ever existed. In Chicago and out here in L.A., you have to have a local person who knows the media and is a specialist in arranging TV and radio appearances. Besides the publicity people at Crown and Warner Books, I've got the services of Jay Allen, who, as I'm sure you know, handled appearances for authors going back to Jacqueline Susann. Out here, Jay Allen has the contacts nobody else has. He said to me, 'I told Merv that none of my clients will go on "The Merv Griffin Show" if there's a Gabor on. Because they steal the time that my client would normally have.' Nobody can make that statement to Merv except Jay Allen. He's retiring from the business any day, but he's handling another appearance of mine this week on Merv Griffin. I'm keyed up now. Tomorrow is my hair day, so I'll be *up* for Merv. Merv does the best plug of all. He holds that book up and he says, '*This* is a *terrific* book; you've *got* to read this book!' Of course, Phil Donahue is the prime, out of Chicago, but the show won't take fiction authors—except Tony Curtis, because he's a movie star, and Gore Vidal, because he's also a political figure. If you wrote a book called *How to Set Your Own Broken Arm,* you could get on Donahue, probably, but if you've written a novel the show doesn't want to know about it. Well, the Griffin show—the first thing in the morning, after I leave the taping, I'll be flying out to Minneapolis-St. Paul, and on to Houston, Dallas, Fort Worth. The treadmill. And then there's 'The Mike Douglas Show' here when I get back. Everybody's out here now. Johnny Carson, Griffin, Douglas—all the talk-show people have moved here. That's why New York is not a good media town anymore—it just takes the network stuff. There's hardly any talk show you can go on from New York, except maybe the 'Today' show, and I got on the 'Today' show the other day from here. I knew I had to convince the 'Today' people that I'd have something fresh to talk about. You can't go on talking about Rodeo Drive forever. As Jay Allen says, 'you don't want to sound like Johnny One-Note.' So I did some research. I knew there was such a thing as compulsive shopping. I talked to a couple of psychoanalysts, a couple of storekeepers about the habits of compulsive buyers. So that's what I talked about on the 'Today' show.''

Mrs. Krantz told me that she was working on the manuscript of a second novel, and had made an outline for it late in 1977, before the hardcover edition of *Scruples* was published. She said she had now written most of the novel itself and expected to finish it that summer. I didn't ask Mrs. Krantz any questions about the novel, and she didn't volunteer any further information about it. However, some time after my talk with her, Janklow told me that the outline was twenty-nine pages long and that after reading it he had taken it to Nat Wartels, the president of Crown, and told him that he had in his possession an outline of another novel by Judith Krantz, "which is going to make *Scruples* look silly," and that he was convinced that "it's going to be a giant book." Janklow said that although he had realized that in submitting an outline for a second Krantz novel at

so early a stage—before the actual publication of *Scruples*—
he might be taking the risk that it would get a less than
clamorous reception, and so might possibly cool some of
the publishers' enthusiasm for Mrs. Krantz's current work,
he decided that he ought to go ahead and show them the
outline. "I'm a lawyer," Janklow said to me. "And I
thought, What's my downside risk in submitting the outline?
It can conform to expectations or it can—let's not say fail,
but succeed in becoming less than a big book. Why not take
the moment when everybody's *anticipating* it'll be a big
book, and move right in and keep the excitement going.
And I must keep it in mind that I'm here not merely to sell
a book but to *orchestrate a career*. My hope was to turn
her into America's premier woman writer of fiction in one
or two books. So I showed the outline to Crown and gave
them the option of buying the book two ways—one a
straight hardcover buy, separate from a paperback buy, and
the other a hard-and-soft buy, which is what they ultimately
decided on. And I gave them a very good price, and they
came back to me and agreed to my terms. Which were a
four-hundred-thousand-dollar advance on the hardcover
edition and an arrangement advantageous to Judy on the
selling of the soft-cover rights. After consulting with me,
Crown took the outline to Warner Books, which had the
right of first refusal on Judy's next book, and asked them
to make a preëmptive bid of a million four hundred thousand
for the paperback rights. But Warner thought that that price
was too high. They told Crown, 'Nobody will pay the kind
of money you're asking, and Janklow doesn't know what
he's doing.' So Crown took the outline to another paperback
house, and *within days* they agreed to give us a *floor* bid
at paperback auction of *a million dollars,* plus three hundred
thousand dollars in bonus clauses.''

At intervals during that summer, I checked with Mrs.
Krantz by long-distance telephone to see how the paperback

edition of *Scruples* and the writing of the new novel were coming along. In answer to the first inquiry, Mrs. Krantz told me that well over three million copies of the paperback edition of *Scruples* were in print. "The only competition *Scruples* has is from outer space," she said. She went on to explain this suggestion of extraterrestrial interference by saying, *"Scruples* has been Number One on the paperback best-seller list for all these weeks, and guess what I've just found out. Now *Alien* is going to be Number One and *Scruples* Number Two. *Alien*—a two-hundred-and-seventy-page piece of schlock! A tie-in novelization, and Warner Books has sold the first million copies of it. A piece of junk! And printed by my own publisher!" Speaking deliberately, she added, "God damn *Alien*. And now I'm Number Two."

On the subject of her novel in progress, she said, "I expect to have it finished soon. It's a good read. It's going to be called *Princess Daisy*. I don't want to be typecast and have people keep asking me how come I know so much about sex. I'm no Joan Didion—there are no intelligent, unhappy people in my books. I want to be known as a writer of good, entertaining narrative. Don't get me wrong. I'm not trying to be taken seriously by the East Coast literary establishment. But I'm taken *very* seriously by the bankers."

Late in July of 1979, I checked by telephone with Janklow in New York on the progress of *Princess Daisy*. Janklow said that the manuscript was completed, that he had read it, and that it was terrific. "We've already got it over to Crown," he told me. "And they *adore* it. Crazy about it. A fabulous book!" Janklow said he was preparing, together with Crown, for a grand auction of the paperback rights to *Princess Daisy* while the book was still in manuscript form. On the basis of the million-dollar floor bid that Crown had obtained, plus the three hundred thousand dollars in bonus clauses attached to it, he was very optimistic, he said, on how high the bidding might go at the actual auction. "I think we'll get *two* million," Janklow said.

On August 30th, Crown sent out copies of a typescript of *Princess Daisy* to the nine major paperback publishers, and, in an accompanying letter, notified them that the auction of the paperback rights to the book would be held on September 12th. The letter, which was signed by Michelle Sidrane, the subsidiary-rights director at Crown, set out in detail the ground rules for bidding at the auction.

"PRINCESS DAISY is bound to be the No. 1 best seller of 1980. A first printing [in hardcover] of 150,000 copies is planned; our initial advertising and promotion budget is set at $150,000.00," the letter said. It then recapitulated "the story of SCRUPLES," including "36 weeks on the New York *Times* Best Seller List, 6 weeks as No. 1 . . . 3 million plus copies in print from Warner Books, the No. 1 mass market best seller during all of Spring 1979 . . . six-hour mini-series from Warner Bros. for CBS . . . for airing February 1980 with a budget of over $6,000,000.00," and ending up with "major British and translation rights deals."

The letter went on to say, "SCRUPLES was a first novel. Now Judith Krantz is established and consequently PRINCESS DAISY will outperform SCRUPLES." To substantiate this promise of superior performance, it informed interested paperback publishers that "Judith Krantz will do full-scale media tours at the time of publication of both the hardcover and paperback editions of PRINCESS DAISY." And by adding that "preparations are under way for a major theatrical motion picture production of PRINCESS DAISY" the letter also seemed to open up to acquisitive paperback people an alluring vision of movie-tie-in sales and, at the appropriate time, a whole third round of promotion, publicity, and—why not?—yet another set of TV- and radio-show tours by the author.

In setting forth the terms for the actual bidding at the

auction, Crown made clear that a floor bid of a million dollars, plus three hundred thousand in bonus clauses, had been established and had already been agreed to by one publisher, whose name the letter did not mention. Under the terms of the auction, the holder of the floor bid would have the opportunity to top by seven and a half per cent the highest offer received at the end of the auction. A number of paragraphs followed concerning the conduct and terms of the auction. One subject dealt with was escalation clauses providing for extra payments based on the book's ranking on the *Times* best-seller list, or if a motion-picture version of *Princess Daisy* was released in theatres or on television. The bidding itself was to be divided into rounds. The bids in the first round were to be blind bids, and the round had to be completed by noon on the day of auction. The bidding order for later rounds was to be determined on the basis of the blind bids; that is, the highest bidder in Round One would have the favored last position in the subsequent rounds. All bids made after Round One were to be made in raises of at least seven and a half per cent over the prior high bid. And the letter concluded, "Sale of the paperback rights is subject to the consent of the author's agent, Morton L. Janklow Associates, Inc."

"I wrote the bidding letter," Janklow told me in a subsequent talk. "We know how to do that better than anyone else. We know how to structure an auction. By structuring your terms for an auction very tightly, you force people to bid in the mode in which you want them to bid. And I like to define the terms in such a way that they are frozen into a bidding formula."

The auction took place as scheduled, with eight of the nine paperback houses that had received the bidding letter participating, the exception being New American Library. The very fact that each of the eight was willing to *start* bidding for the paperback rights to the as yet unpublished novel at more than a million dollars clearly indicated the ultimate stakes involved in competitive paperback marketing—especially, one might suppose, since in the months between the time when I first heard about Judith Krantz's forthcoming second novel and the date of the auction the paperback market in general was said to have "softened," although to a lesser extent than business as a whole in this country. Of course, the people at Crown would look upon all the big money ready to be thrown in (after all, the eight publishers' participation in the auction meant that a bare minimum of eight million dollars had been set aside simply to cover the openers) as a huge vote of confidence in the worth of *Princess Daisy,* and so would Janklow. Still, in a talk I had with Janklow shortly before the day of the auction he predicted that the very softening of the paperback market over the previous few months would drive the price eventually paid for the paperback rights to *Princess Daisy* up rather than down, because, he argued, the competing publishers would be all the more eager to capture a potential blockbuster, which might achieve or preserve for their whole current book line a dominant position in the racks of the paperback outlets across the country.

On the day of the auction, as on the days immediately preceding it, everybody connected with the affair appeared tense. No outsiders were allowed in or near the scene of the auction, at Crown headquarters; even Janklow was stationed physically apart from Crown's offices, although he was in constant touch with the Crown people by telephone. Nobody at Crown was talking to the press, and even Janklow had no comment for the time being. The reason for all the secrecy was the same as that at any auction involving large sums of money: the participants wanted to play their cards as close to the vest as possible. The Crown people knew that they would be dealing with thoroughly experienced bidders, determined to prevent the escape of information that might afford their competition any insight into the characteristics or patterns of their bidding practices. Added to these considerations was the fact that this was the first really big-time paperback-rights auction for Michelle Sidrane as Crown's subsidiary-rights director.

The auction was conducted entirely by telephone. It began at nine in the morning, and the first of the blind bids was telephoned by Mrs. Sidrane at five minutes past nine. The bid was for a million one hundred thousand dollars, plus the bonus money in the escalation clauses. It was followed by bids for a million five, a million five hundred and twenty-five thousand, and another of a million five. Then, between eleven-fifteen and eleven-forty-five, there were three bids for a million one hundred thousand. "This was just to establish who was going to be in the game," Janklow explained a day or two after the auction. The blind bidding that morning did not proceed without flareups, I learned, and even in the glowing aftermath of the auction Janklow seemed to feel a bit stirred by what had happened. Without mentioning the names of either the people or the publishing houses involved, he gave me an account of one incident. "During the blind-bidding round, the chief executive and the chief operating officer of one of the major paperback houses called me," he said. "First, they had called Crown, and Crown had told them to clear it with me. They placed a bid that was very high, but under conditions not provided for in the bidding letter. They wanted to give that high bid, but without the bonuses provided for in the escalation clauses. I said, 'I can't accept that bid, high as it is, because it deviates from the terms laid down for the auction.' They said—and I quote—'You're a God-damned fool. You don't know what you're doing, and you're screwing up this auction.' I said to the chairman of this company, 'Listen, one thing I'm not is a fool, and tomorrow we can discuss who's right and who's wrong, and in the meantime we'll play the game according to *my* rules. If I change the rules now, I have to go back and re-advise all the other parties and give them the opportunity to restructure their bids.' The chairman said to me, 'You mean you're passing up this bid of a million and a half dollars?' I said I was. They said they were going to drop out of the auction. I said, 'I'm sorry, I'm not going to accept your bid under these conditions.' Lots of screaming and yelling. I said, 'Why shouldn't you bid the way I suggested two weeks ago that everybody bid? Why wait till today?' There was a long pause, and then one of them said to me, 'We don't like playing the game by the rules *you* set. We want to play the game by the rules *we* set.' I said, 'That's not a reason, that's an excuse. Now I'm really not going to do anything, and that's it, and goodbye!' I called Nat Wartels at Crown, and I told him, 'I think they're bluffing and they'll come back in.' "

Notwithstanding the firmness of his goodbye, Janklow soon was talking again to the chairman and the chief executive officer of that publishing house. He told me, "I said to them, 'Look, if you're willing to bid a million five, then bid a million two hundred thousand and bonuses.' 'We don't want to do that.' I told them, 'This is the trend of arrogance that has cost a lot in this industry. I'm not going to give in.' So at twelve noon on the stroke these people called in the bid I wanted, and they continued right through the auction as one of the major bidders. A classic example of inflexibility. A refusal to do things just because someone else set the rules. There were three or four of these episodes during the day, where we had to take risks. In one of the later rounds, for example, one of the major players couldn't come in with a bid for a couple of hours, because the senior corporation executives weren't there. We waited and waited. I said 'Someone should be available.' Crown said, 'Well, we can't shut them out on the ground of time.' We waited, waited, and I said, 'That's it! They've got fifteen minutes! If they don't get their bid in by three-thirty, we're going on to the next round—it's not fair to the others.' We delivered that message. God, such consternation! So it becomes a war of nerves. I happen to be competent at playing in that war. Look at that episode in the morning. They'd had that bidding letter dated August 30th—why the hell raise this in the middle of an auction on September 12th? The point is, people think that by upsetting the auctioneer they can obtain an advantage. Which is why I like to retain control over decisions at an auction. Well, we delivered that message in midafternoon that the other bidder had fifteen minutes. And at three-thirty *right on the button* they came in with their bid.

"After the conclusion of the blind-bidding round, we already knew we had a *very* big auction. Then we went on with Round Two. Now, the rules called for the highest bidder in Round One to get the last spot in Round Two, and for each bid to exceed the previous high bid by seven and a half per cent. So the maker of the lowest bid in Round One was the first bidder in Round Two. All right. The people who finally made that three-thirty bid deadline came in with a one-million-seven-hundred-and-fifty-thousand-dollar bid. Then another house was approached by Crown and invited to bid. They told us they passed. They told us their top had been a million four. Then the next house that was approached also said this was too rich for them and they were getting out. Remember, topping a million seven-fifty by seven and a half per cent meant that the bid was like a million eight-eight for the next bidder. To stay in Round Two, they now had to be bidding at a level almost as high as for any book rights sold in history. Very interesting! That was one reason for staging the incremental bids at seven and a half per cent, because I had seen all these people in major auctions and I knew how slowly it could go. I sold a book a couple of months ago for five hundred and sixty-one thousand dollars, and it took two days, and they were bidding up in five-thousand-dollar increments. So you *force* their attention. There's nothing like a hanging to attract the attention of the hangee! If they're not going to be serious players—unless they're *really* prepared—they *ought* to get out. Requiring these sizable increments in the bidding also enabled me to close out the auction that day. Because I don't like the overnight hiatus—the people get nervous, they go home, they can't sleep, get cramps, maybe get to thinking they shouldn't be in this after all. The whole purpose of an auction is to get a momentum, drive it forward, and maintain it, so people don't start falling by the wayside—it's like a real-estate deal. Real-estate lawyers say, 'Close the deal if you stay till four in the morning. Don't let people change their minds.'

"Well, so we had three passes in a row. Then, at five o'clock, one of the major houses—the same one that had given us that trouble in Round One on that disparate bid— now came and said they'd be prepared to make a very substantial bid if we were prepared to deal without the three hundred thousand in bonuses, just deal with straight money. And they would agree to accelerate the payments. Money being what it is, that was very important. At this level and at available interest rates of fourteen, fifteen per cent, if you can manage to get your money a year earlier, it's a fortune for you. So at this point we went back to the floor bidder and said we'd like an opportunity to change the rules, and I felt we could change them, because there were now so few players left in the auction. The floor bidder agreed to the change of rules. So we went back to the other players and got everybody's approval of the rule change. So the house that had proposed the straight-money bid without the bonuses but with accelerated payments now made a bid of two million four, with no bonuses but with the accelerated-payment provision. Somewhere about six-thirty, the next-highest house topped that bid, and bid two million five-eighty. We were now well over the world's record price for paperback rights—more than the two and a quarter million dollars that Fawcett paid for *Linda Goodman's Love Signs,* more than the two million five-fifty that N.A.L. paid for Mario Puzo's *Fools Die,* which included three hundred thousand dollars for the rights to reprint *The Godfather.*

"So we went into Round Three. Crown went back to the house that had first bid a million seven-fifty. Their bid had to be two million five-eighty, plus the increment of seven and a half per cent. They passed. So we went to a second bidder and we got a bid of two million seven-seventy-three and five hundred. Then we went back to the previous bidder. They were ready to advance beyond the previous bid, but came with a whole different set of conditions as to the payment schedule. And by stretching the payment schedule what they'd be doing was buying the use of money. And that would cost my client Judy Krantz *money.* And I rejected that bid. They said, 'We're not going to go on, then.' And I said, 'I hate to lose you.' Bluffed them out. And at the last second, at about eight-forty-five, they came back and made that same bid but without the stretchout. The bid was for two million nine-eighty-five."

That bid came from Ballantine Books. The earlier two-million-four-hundred-thousand bid had been made by Warner Books. That was just a million dollars more than the sum for which, in December of 1977, Crown had offered Warner Books the rights to *Princess Daisy*—an offer Warner had turned down. Warner's bid at the auction twenty-one months later was probably intended as what is known in these auctions as a knockout bid—one representing a high enough jump over previous bids to discourage the competition from further bidding. But when Warner was outbid in turn, it was the Warner people who became discouraged. And they dropped out after one more bid. With Ballantine now the high bidder, Nat Wartels, at Crown, decided, after consulting with Janklow, that the time had come for Crown to inform the supposedly secret floor bidder waiting in the wings—actually, by that time the floor bidder was known by most of the other parties to be Bantam Books—of the Ballantine bid. Shortly after nine o'clock, Michelle Sidrane telephoned the Bantam people and informed them of the situation, and said that unless they decided to exercise their privilege of topping the Ballantine figure by seven and a half per cent the paperback rights to *Princess Daisy* would go to Ballantine.

"Normally, the topping by the floor bidder in an auction is a very quick part of the deal," Janklow told me later. "All the floor bidder usually has to say at that point is yes or no. But that's not how it was at this auction. The worst part of the auction, as far as I was concerned, followed that call. I'd been in my office, and on the phone, since a quarter of nine that morning, and when it looked as though things were close to the end I went home for a shower and a shave. My wife and I had been invited to a black-tie dinner on the upper East Side, so I left for the party and sat down at dinner. A very lovely party. People from the social world and the diplomatic corps were there. It was given by Alice Mason, who is a real-estate woman. Mayor Koch was there, Barbara Walters was there, lots of diplomats, lots of pals of mine were there, Sally Quinn, of the Washington *Post,* was there. After six or seven minutes and two bites of my dinner, the hostess's daughter came in and said there was a phone call for me. I left the table and took the call in a bedroom, from which I didn't return for three hours. Long-drawn-out negotiations on conference calls with Crown, with Bantam. The people at Bantam said they were going to exercise their topping privilege, but they raised questions about their getting certain rights and options in connection with Judy Krantz's next book, which is not yet written and has been offered to nobody. We discussed all that in call after call, for hour after hour. And I kept Judy, who was in Beverly Hills, informed of the progress, too. This was an orchestration that had begun a long time ago, and it started with a wonderful book. Judy is a very smart woman, and this is her life, her career, and her money, and when I was taking these relatively risky positions, rejecting bids and so on, during the auction, I always checked with her. I must have spoken to her fifteen times that day. You can't do that with every client. But Judy understands the marketing process. She wants to know just what the situation is, and I enjoy having her know. Well, about Bantam, in talking to these people in the conference calls I kept backing them down and backing them down, and about twenty of twelve we all came to an agreement on terms.''

And so, in an auction that lasted fourteen and a half hours, and for three million two hundred thousand dollars in round figures ($3,208,875, to be precise), the paperback rights to *Princess Daisy* went to Bantam Books—whose former chairman had complained to me only a few months previously that the "frantic bidding" and "outlandish" prices being paid for paperback rights to potential best-sellers were detrimental to the best interests of the book-publishing industry in general and were contributing to a situation in which "books of quality and of superior interest are being shoved off the stands."

News of the outcome of the auction made front pages all over the country. The front-page report in the *Times* on September 14th was headlined, "A RECORD $3.2 MILLION IS PLEDGED BY BANTAM FOR NEW KRANTZ NOVEL." Each of the big three national TV and radio networks carried a report on Bantam's acquisition, and stressed the record price paid for the rights. For Bantam, Janklow, and Mrs. Krantz, it was a heartwarming situation, since the news engendered by the giant price paid was probably worth, in the equivalent of paid advertising (and without Crown's having yet spent more than a small part of even the hundred and fifty thousand dollars allocated to promotion of the hardcover edition of the yet to be published book), even more than the three million two hundred thousand dollars actually committed for the paperback rights to *Princess Daisy*.

At Farrar, Straus & Giroux, the comment of Roger Straus to me right after the news of Bantam's record purchase was "It's revolting." Of course, Straus hadn't *read Princess Daisy*. Nor had anyone else, really, except the Crown people, and those at the paperback houses, each of which had then bid at least a million three hundred thousand dollars for it. In all the publicity stirred up over the price of the book, its actual theme and content appeared as a matter of minor interest, though a news release from Crown, headed "New Krantz Novel Sold for Record-Shattering Figure," did quote the Crown editor-in-chief, Carole Baron, as noting, "It is full of fabulous characters, European aristocrats, glamorous women, American television and business personalities, and a heroine, Princess Daisy, who appears destined to capture the imagination of the reading and movie-going public. Ms. Krantz has cemented her position as America's most popular novelist."

The day after the auction, Mrs. Krantz told me, by telephone from Beverly Hills, "I'm on top of the world. The phone has been ringing like mad. In my heart of hearts, I know they are right to pay more." Bantam, she meant. "There aren't any good reads out. The new Norman Mailer book, *The Executioner's Song,* isn't a good read. *Princess Daisy* is 'the book I wish I had on a weekend.' That's the secret of it. Women feel that way. Plus I have a large male audience. During the auction, my husband said to me, 'You're unnaturally calm.' I sat around and ate turkey wings and ironed the wrinkles out of my clothes; I'd just got back from a vacation in Europe. Morty Janklow was in touch with me constantly, but I never phoned him. Morty did a most brilliant job. He was like a ringmaster. Handled the whole thing like handling tigers, and absolutely firm. Mario Puzo had the record up to now—two million five-fifty. Now *Princess Daisy* is the world record. I'm the most highly paid first novelist and the most highly paid second novelist in the world. Of course, they'd told me a year ago about Bantam's million-dollar commitment on *Princess Daisy*. I must say there were mornings at the typewriter during those months when I thought of that floor bid.''

Naturally, newspapers all over ran items about the triumphant price obtained for the paperback rights to *Princess Daisy*. And *People* ran a big feature story on the subject, with a full-page picture captioned, in the upper-left-hand corner, "The Price Went Up-Up-Up-Sa Daisy to $3.2 Million for the New Novel by the Author of *Scruples.*" The picture showed Mrs. Krantz, wearing a bath towel and apparently nothing else, sitting cross-legged in a sauna and reading *The Letters of Virginia Woolf.* A subcaption at the bottom left of the picture explained, "Krantz takes to the sauna with some highbrow reading.''

A bit later on, when I caught up with Mrs. Krantz in New York, she told me of *People*'s coverage of her career as a novelist. "When *Scruples* became Number One, *People* took a million pictures of me at home, a lot of them with my husband and me together. We had to climb into a bed together and read. I had all my clothes on under a bathrobe that they had me wear. These photographers like to set things up. I remember that after *Scruples* had been Number One for a while *Newsweek* was going to have a cover story on best-selling authors. Sidney Sheldon was supposed to be on the cover, and *Newsweek* sent a photographer around who spent a lot of time taking pictures of me. But the test-tube baby was born and the Pope died, and the cover story became a back-of-the-book story and came out a bit later. It had pictures of Sidney Sheldon and Irving Wallace and his family, and Harold Robbins on the Riviera, and me at home. They'd photographed me sitting in the corner of a sofa and holding a big goblet in my hand. They'd said to me, 'Put something in a glass that looks alcoholic.' Actually, what I put in the glass was iced tea. The way it came out, it looked as though I were drinking my way into oblivion.

"Well, after the *Princess Daisy* auction, *People* sent over an ex-*Life* photographer to my house. He kept saying things like, 'This shot is kind of dull' and 'This is a sort of boring shot' and 'Don't you people do anything interesting?' Steve said, 'Well, I jog.' He said, 'No, we don't want a jogging shot.' Well, we're not skin divers or anything. Most of the time, after all, I'm just sitting at the typewriter. Steve told him, 'We have a stationary bike upstairs.' The photographer wanted to get me in leotards on the bicycle. I said, 'No leotard shots.' Well, we happened to have bought a house with a sauna, which we don't use. The *People* photographer said, 'Put on a big bath towel and bring up a book. We'll shoot you in the sauna, reading.' By that time, after four hours of picture-taking, I was getting to be like a punch-drunk prizefighter. So I did what he asked me. He had me put on a big bath towel over my underwear, and I took a book of Virginia Woolf's letters I'd been reading—I happen to be a Bloomsbury freak—and let him pose me in that sauna. And so I learned something important—that if you ever pose for a magazine in an unlikely position, *that's* the shot they're going to use."

And thereby, in the case of this particular shot and the accompanying story, help strengthen, if ever so modestly, the golden link between the circulation of *People* and the cause of the big book, and so intensify the exploitable American reveries of celebrity, media respect, big money. The issue of *People* containing the article on Judith Krantz and the record price for the paperback rights to *Princess Daisy* was the featured subject of a full-page ad that appeared on the back page of the *Times* and other newspapers. The ad reproduced, very prominently, the picture of Mrs. Krantz in her literary-sauna pose, and the picture had a new caption underneath. It now read, "Novelist Judith Krantz may not be Tolstoy but she can boil a plot. Her not-yet-published *Princess Daisy* just fetched $3.2 million for paperback rights—the highest price in history for a mere book. Will life change? Heck no. Husband Steve made millions from flicks. . . . They've been rich for years." The themes of celebrity and big money were also prominent in descriptions within the same ad of other articles featured in that issue of *People*. Alongside a closeup of the clothes designer Bonnie Cashin was a copy block saying, "Bonnie Cashin is still cashin' in on her classic look. She's designed costumes for some 60 films, won five Coty Awards, invented ponchos for women and the layered look, grossed $25 million last year." And alongside a picture of the basketball player Ann Meyers in action on the court the copy said, "All-American Ann Meyers got $50,000 for signing with the Indiana Pacers. But the 140-pounder couldn't hack it with all those male giants." The lower part of the ad described the informational contributions of *People*. "*People*'s where you learn what's doing in the world through the people who are doing the doing . . . nobody pins down the movers and shakers and makers like *People*," it declared, and, in an aside to *Times* readers with Madison Avenue interests, it pointed out, concerning the "so many millions of today's people" who "can't wait to jump into every week's *People*," that "they're an advertiser's dream . . . active, educated, prospering, with-it women and men" and "they're into the 1980s *now*." And as for *People* itself, it is "where the 1980s are already happening" and "it is the super-*hu-*

man selling environment."

In the meantime, I had been back to see Janklow at his office. He was still in a good mood. "Today, I was down at Crown for two and a half hours discussing the foreign-rights sales to *Princess Daisy*," he told me. "I've been getting calls from people about the English rights. Crown and I will make an English sale that will be a record sale, and when we come back from the International Book Fair in Frankfurt next month we will have *cleaned up* the foreign market. We'll have German, Spanish, French, Italian, Scandinavian sales that will all be record-breakers." So far, the foreign hardcover and paperback rights to *Princess Daisy* have totalled two million dollars. Naturally, Janklow said, the foreign-rights sales of the book had been spurred enormously by the unprecedented price obtained at the auction for the American paperback rights. "It's an extraordinary tribute to *Princess Daisy* to have seen so many players participating at that level," he said. "Normally, you'll get only two or three players in the bidding stratosphere."

Only five days after the *Princess Daisy* auction, another book-rights auction had been held, in which Simon & Schuster's Summit Books Division auctioned off the rights to Marilyn French's *The Bleeding Heart* for a million nine hundred and ten thousand dollars. The victorious bidder had been Ballantine Books, the next-to-highest bidder for the *Princess Daisy* rights. I suggested to Janklow a short time later that the high price obtained for *The Bleeding Heart* might have represented in part a kind of momentum from the *Princess Daisy* auction, in that the money that had been allocated by the unsuccessful contestants for the capture of the *Princess Daisy* rights was already on hand for bidding at the next major book auction. Janklow agreed emphatically. *"We made that auction. We made that one-million-nine price!"* he declared. He was referring to the

Marilyn French auction. "Right after the *Princess Daisy* auction, I not only predicted the level at which the Marilyn French book would go—I also predicted who would get it. I said, 'Ballantine is sitting on just about three million dollars that they didn't spend on *Princess Daisy*—they'll be the buyer. And I believe we made that Marilyn French auction because we'd shown the paperback business that it wasn't in such a soft market after all. I also think that the Judy Krantz book at three-million-two-oh-eight is a much better buy than the French book at a million nine. With *Princess Daisy,* we demonstrated that the market is not soft for quality books. The paperback market needs these leaders more than ever now. With just so many racks at the retail outlets these nine houses are in violent competition with each other for space on the shelf. This is a situation requiring the full use of marketing capacity. My opinion is that Procter & Gamble could hire a smart acquisitions editor and go into the paperback business tomorrow. If I owned the Hanes Corporation, which owns L'Eggs panty hose, *I* would buy a paperback house, because the two businesses have essentially the same distribution pattern. The same salesman who carries my panty hose into the drugstores and supermarkets and railroad and bus stations and airport terminals is walking directly up to the rack where the paperbacks are being sold, and I remember noticing at an Eastern Airlines terminal when I was flying to Florida a while back a rack of paperbacks and a rack of panty hose, one on top of the other. Remember that these leaders, like *Princess Daisy,* not only capture the space on the racks but help the rest of the publisher's line get it. If you walked into a paperback outlet last spring looking for *Scruples,* you might see a paperback rack with forty-eight slots, and eight of them would contain copies of *Scruples*—the whole top rack filled with *Scruples.* That was worth a tremendous amount to Warner and the whole Warner line. And when

Bantam is due to go in, during March of 1981, with *Princess Daisy,* the effect of this book will be like— Do you remember that political leader in New York years ago who once talked about Franklin Roosevelt, and said, 'He's like the Staten Island Ferry; when he pulls into the slip all the garbage comes in with him'? And when that Bantam salesman walks into that Okefenokee supermarket and the guy's got forty-eight spots on his rack and the salesman has this *giant, record* book, that Bantam guy is going to get a lot of shelf space for all kinds of Bantam books."

In anticipation of the day when the Bantam salesman would walk in with the giant, record book, Janklow was already preparing the orchestration of further passages in the Judith Krantz literary career. "Movies—we've had inquiries from just about every studio and independent on *Princess Daisy,"* he told me. "We have not made a decision yet. The only decision made is that Steve Krantz himself is going to produce it. One woman, a Hollywood scriptwriter, called me. She said it left her breathless—the best book she'd read since *The Thorn Birds*—and she said it'll be a fabulous movie. We have Michael Ovitz"—the Hollywood deal-maker—"and his boys working on it. They've just finished reading *Princess Daisy* over the weekend. They had a staff meeting, which we joined by conference call, about the variety of approaches possible in the dramatic sales. Michael is meeting with the Krantzes. We can sell it with Steve in the package as producer for a big amount of money and a big percentage of the gross. That's my least preferred way. Or we can put elements in it—put a line producer under Steve, put in a writer, a director, maybe a star or two, then package it ourselves, present it to a studio in a completed or semicompleted package, which tends to increase the value a lot. We can go so far, if we choose, as to independently finance it. There's nothing to stop us from going to NBC now and selling for seven or eight million dollars the rights to the as yet unmade movie, and then going to Home Box Office or Viacom and selling them the syndication rights after television, then taking that money and going to a German or Canadian tax-shelter group and getting the rest of the financing, and financing the picture on our own, and making it, and then going to Paramount and saying, 'You can have eighteen per cent to distribute it.' We'll make our decision as to just how to go in in our own good time. We don't have a book''—the hardcover edition of *Princess Daisy*—''till March, and we don't have the paperback publication due till March of 1981, so we're eighteen months away from the paperback as we sit here. The timing has to be right. The paperback should have its own run, and then there will be the movie, and that will give the paperback of *Princess Daisy* its second life. *Scruples* is going to have a second life in paperback after the hardcover publication of *Princess Daisy,* because that will send further huge numbers of people to buy *Scruples*. And *Scruples* will begin yet *another* life in paperback this coming February, when the six-hour mini-series based on the book goes on television. That's in production now. The most expensive movie per hour on television ever made. When that movie goes on television, we'll sell a further million and a half copies of *Scruples* in paperback. That timing is all set. In the meantime, I'm getting ready to set the periodical-serial sales for the hardcover of *Princess Daisy*. I have three interested magazines, and I have told them they're going to have to pay a hundred thousand dollars or more for the serial rights. And they're begging for a look at the manuscript. I want the cover of *Ladies' Home Journal,* or whatever, for March, because the issue dated March will go on the stands in February, and while the book itself has a March publication date the books will actually be in the bookstores by the end of January or the first week in February.''

We discussed the economics of the publication and sale of the paperback edition of *Princess Daisy*. Just after the auction of the paperback rights, the Bantam people had estimated that they would have to print between four million and six million copies of *Princess Daisy* in order to recoup the three million two hundred thousand dollars paid out as an advance—the exact number of copies depending on the price at which Bantam decided to sell it. Janklow told me that since *Princess Daisy* would be more than five hundred pages in paperback, he believed that the price Bantam would set would probably be three dollars and fifty cents a copy. Janklow picked up a trade newsletter from his desk and read me an item saying that sales of mass-market paperbacks had risen four and a half per cent in the first six months of 1979. Then he said, "And here they've been screaming about a soft market, and all the big prices they have to pay for book rights. It shows you what a nickel-and-dime business this is. The big paperback publishers like to talk poor. Look, suppose they plan to put *Princess Daisy* on sale at three-fifty a copy and then they get a pulp-cost increase—they'll just add another quarter on the price. What do you think it costs now to print four and a half million copies of *Princess Daisy* in paperback? With the glossy cover? In runs of a million? Thirteen and a half cents a copy! There's a *gigantic* swing between cost and profit when you get into huge printings, and the fact that the paperback publishers are crying poor is to affect *me* as much as anyone else. Now, there's a lot of incremental cost involved, sure. Suppose the book is going to sell at just three dollars. Most authors get a royalty of ten per cent; I see that mine get fifteen. (And my author, for *Princess Daisy,* gets to keep seventy per cent of the paperback proceeds— not fifty or sixty, as most authors do.) That's forty-five cents right off the top from Book One sold. The distributor will get a discount of between forty-seven and fifty-two per cent of the retail price, so Bantam is selling *Princess Daisy* to the distributor for a dollar-fifty. Then the distributor has to give the retailer a discount. Where does the other dollar-fifty go? Bantam has that dollar-fifty, less the author's royalty. That means that Bantam is left with a dollar and five cents. It's got promotion, it's got corporate overhead, it's got to contend with returns. Do you realize that there are many paperback books that come back to the publisher in the *unopened* cartons in which they've been shipped out, and that not only does the paperback house have to credit them but it's got to pay shipment to and from the retailer? Getting the books onto the shelves, getting them *moving*—that's what the business is about. And it pays to have some big books to do that. On a lot of paperback titles, the returns can average thirty or thirty-five per cent, and they can go as high as fifty per cent. But I say that there will be *far fewer* returns on *Princess Daisy,* and that's what's going to make a big difference. Do you know what happens when the returns go down from fifty per cent to only twenty per cent? The difference all goes to the *bottom line,* because it's *all profit*—the paper's been paid for, the transportation's been paid for. So any time you can show me a business where I can pay thirteen cents for a product, and have a dollar-five or ten or fifteen gross profit before expenses, that's a good business. And, as to how good a business it is, I'll give you the whole history of modern book publishing in two sentences. Just four years ago, Charles Bluhdorn, the chief executive of Gulf & Western Industries, *brilliantly* acquired Simon & Schuster, its backlist, Pocket Books, Fireside Books, all its imprints, its furniture, equipment—the whole thing, lock, stock, and barrel—for ten and a half million dollars. And four years later I've got almost *one-third* of that amount for the paperback-reprint rights for seven years in North America to *one novel.*"

CHAPTER 14

Some
Misunderstandings

THE EXTRAORDINARY transformation of the American book-publishing industry from what was once, for the most part, a diverse group of independently owned concerns into subordinate divisions of corporate conglomerates has undoubtedly had many effects whose nature has not been fully comprehended even by people who make their living in the business, and there does not seem to be any reason to believe that they might necessarily have been better comprehended by people in, say, government. During the past few years, however, the wave of mergers and the increasing concentration of publishing houses in the hands of a few conglomerates or large communications companies have drawn the attention of various governmental agencies concerned with the enforcement of the anti-trust laws. As a result of one federal investigation, the Justice Department in 1978 brought an anti-trust suit against CBS, charging that CBS (whose share in the paperback-publishing business up to 1977 had consisted of ownership of Popular Library), by acquiring the major mass-market-paperback house Fawcett Publications, had taken an action that might substantially lessen competition or tend to create a monopoly in the mass-market-paperback business. That litigation is at present in a pre-trial stage. Again, for some months the Federal Trade Commission has been investigating the acquisition of the Book-of-the-Month Club by Time, Inc., in 1977, to determine whether or not that may be in violation of the Clayton Anti-Trust Act. Further, the F.T.C. is known to be in the preliminary stages of a broad investigation into the book-publishing business as a whole, with special attention to trade practices that might be construed as restricting fair competition in the industry. And, yet further, a subcommittee on anti-trust, monopoly, and business rights of the Senate Judiciary Committee has been holding hearings concerning concentration in the book-publishing and bookselling industries. Just what is likely to come out of all these inquiries is an open question. It could be that some specific regulatory measures will eventually be taken—concerning, for example, the ownership by one conglomerate of competing subsidiaries or segments in book publishing, or concerning book-distribution practices—which will have the effect of increasing competition within some areas of the industry, but it seems unlikely that such specific measures will materially affect the prevailing course of increasing concentration in the business as a whole. The rate of mergers and conglomerate acquisitions of publishing houses might slow in relation to the rate during the past decade, but there certainly does not appear to be any foreseeable end to these big-company acquisitions, let alone a reversal of the trend. And it must be noted that the big wave of mergers and sales of independent family-owned book houses took place in large part because the federal estate tax put huge difficulties in the way of planning and carrying out an orderly and rational transition from one generation of publishing-house proprietors to another. Unfortunately, governmental action now hardly seems likely to remedy a situation that government policies helped to bring about in the first instance. Perhaps the best that can be hoped for in this area is that the government can be brought to restrain actions by its own agencies which tend to increase rather than decrease concentration in the publishing industry—for example, the I.R.S. ruling that publishers are not entitled to tax write-downs on books held in inventory, a ruling that will unquestionably have the effect of encouraging publishers to clear out from their inventories books that have less than spectacular sales, and thus of escalating even further the current emphasis on blockbuster books.

The controversy over conglomerate ownership and control in the book industry has often been debated with such passion that a lot of the facts at issue have become somewhat obscured. Not all aspects of the existing panorama are necessarily as dark as they are apt to appear to the more vehement opponents of the conglomerate role in book publishing. For example, there have been widespread fears that conglomerate control of publishing houses will result in some kind of censorship or backstage blacklisting of books critical of or abhorrent to the political or economic outlook of the conglomerates concerned. It is possible that this is occurring, but I have come across no evidence of it. Indeed, in the present period of conglomerate ownership of publishing houses there may actually be less direct censorship or refusal to deal with politically unwelcome ideas than existed in family-owned independent publishing houses, because these were often run in a manner that was not only idiosyncratic but peremptory. According to A. Scott Berg's biography of Maxwell Perkins, the rumor around Charles Scribner's Sons after Ernest Hemingway submitted the manuscript of *The Sun Also Rises* was that Charles Scribner, the president of the house, had such strenuous objections to the work because of its frank language concerning sexual matters that only a threat of resignation by Perkins induced him to agree to publish it (and that even then many of those references had to be eliminated or toned down by the author before the book was actually published). And it might be worthwhile to recall that George Orwell's masterpiece of political satire *Animal Farm* was turned down by several houses before it was finally accepted for publication in Britain, and also turned down by three publishers in this country before it was accepted by Harcourt, Brace. That refusal to deal with the ideas of a remarkable writer was a result not of big-business pressure but, rather, of the reluctance of people in the independently owned American publishing houses, who were generally very liberal, to take on a book so bitingly critical of the Stalinist regime at a time when the expression of anti-Stalinist sentiments was often regarded as dubiously motivated propaganda likely to interfere with postwar Soviet-American relations.

So far, then, the imputations of incipient conglomerate political censorship appear to be unfounded. But if a manuscript, political or nonpolitical, fiction or nonfiction, comes in to a present-day conglomerate publishing division and is seen as one to which the paperback rights can't be sold off before it ever gets out of manuscript form, that is another matter. The rejection of such a manuscript is never considered to be the result of conglomerate censorship or interference with the free flow of ideas. It is merely a decision by acquisitions editors and subsidiary-rights directors—all of whom are only too well aware of their accountability to the corporate bottom line for their individual "performance"—as to how well the book appears to fit into an overall big-book marketing plan. And if the negative decision is passed off to the author involved as the result of considered editorial judgment of his or her book's intrinsic artistic merit, the rejection cannot be called censorship, perhaps, but the result for the author is just as unhappy.

Another aspect of conglomerate control of contemporary

book publishing which may be incompletely understood has to do with the assumption by many of its critics that conglomerate common ownership of motion-picture companies and record companies as well as book-publishing companies means that various corporate arms of particular conglomerates are going in for a great deal of quiet inside trading with one another—that movie rights, television rights, recording rights, paperback-reprint rights to a particular book are being jointly developed and exploited by the various divisions of a single conglomerate, the effect being to keep the book out of a truly open market. It may very well be that such "basketing" of hardcover, paperback, movie, and other rights within the divisions of conglomerates or big communications companies was envisioned as an important part of the grandiose corporate "synergy" projected in the big conglomerate expansion during the past decade or more. But on the whole things don't seem to have worked out that way. While the people in the paperback division and movie-production division of a conglomerate often do get an inside track on the content and availability of commercially desirable works from the hardcover-book division, and while that often makes for a competitive advantage to the divisions of the conglomerate, it does not assure that the various rights to the works are going to wind up being owned by those divisions. For a division to get advance knowledge of the availability of rights to a work does not necessarily mean that it buys them. While there certainly may be some of this kind of inside trading, I have been unable so far to discern any general pattern of favoritism between divisions of conglomerates concerning the sale of subsidiary rights to hardcover books—a pattern indicating, for example, that the movie-production division of a conglomerate is regularly selling movie-tie-in publication rights to the paperback-publishing arm of the same conglomerate. However, several hardcover and paperback publishers I have talked to do concede that pressure from the management of conglomerates on their divisions to engage in special deals that have the flavor of inside trading is a possibility they always have to reckon with. Oscar Dystel, of Bantam, said of that possibility, "We're watching the situation very carefully." Certainly it seems that the power grabbing and restraint of free commerce that could arise through this kind of inside dealmaking is something to be taken seriously and monitored closely.

In any event, the fact that this sort of inside trading hasn't developed isn't necessarily ascribable to any inherent shyness on the part of conglomerate managements about giving their divisions inside advantages. Rather, what has inhibited them most seems to be the vastly increased power of at least some authors' agents, whose ability to grasp control of literary and other rights is something that the conglomerates had not reckoned with in expanding their communications empires. And it seems an ironic circumstance that conglomerates in the publishing business should be held back from further exercise of their economic power largely by agents who, by exacting ever-higher prices for big-book hardcover and paperback-reprint rights, have themselves helped to escalate the blockbuster wars—wars that have had profoundly distressing effects on authors who may be writers of considerable literary worth but whose works are not considered compatible with big-book publishing practices. A rather slender reed against which to lean the integrity of contemporary American literature, it seems.

On the current book-publishing scene, there still are many small, independent publishers of specialized books in hardcover form. And an entrepreneur needs to have no very large amount of capital on hand to enter this business, because once he has a promising manuscript in his possession he can subcontract the design of the book, choose a printer, and make an arrangement with an existing publishing house to use its sales-and-distribution system to get the book sent around to the bookstores. Then, there are editors who, stepping aside from regular staff employment at a publishing house, elect to make special profit-sharing arrangements with that publisher or another—arrangements in which the publisher puts out under the editor's imprint books that the editor has acquired. In a way, the juggernaut advance of big-book publishing may have given special impetus to the more ingenious and spirited of those editors, since comparatively few manuscripts and authors are considered to be in the big-book league; and some of the better university presses have similarly benefitted from the availability of manuscripts of merit that the big conglomerate-owned houses are not interested in touching.

But all these activities considered together are hardly likely to affect the course of big-company, big-deal, big-book publishing. Richard Snyder, of Simon & Schuster, predicted some time ago that concentration in the book-publishing industry would probably continue until most of the industry is under the control of a few large corporations, "like the seven sisters of the oil business." If he is right, one can estimate the effectiveness of future governmental regulatory action to slow the trend by what the government has done to control the seven sisters in the oil business. In any event, something else seems to be involved in what has happened to the book business—a force that is fused with and yet extends beyond conglomerate power itself. That combine might be called the siren sisters of hype. By that I mean the ever-increasing power that can be marshalled and focussed in the communications-and-publishing business through the manipulation of all the diverse and highly interactive elements of modern mass-merchandising, advertising, and promotion techniques to attain commercial ends—a force that large organizations, power combinations in themselves, have come to understand and invoke. It is hype that seizes what is exploitable and dismisses what is not. Hype expresses its ideals in the exaltation of large numbers—in numbers of copies peddled, audiences reached, prices demanded and paid, dollar records broken and broken again. Of all the large numbers, the largest, most celebrated in hype is also the smallest: Number One. Number One is the star buildup by the well-plotted campaign to reach the magic threshold where the mass media, having been the target of the hype, accept the newsworthiness of the subject and actually become supplicants for the subject's time and attention.

Given the big-time, big-money, winner-take-all system so evident in the movie industry, the television industry (including the television news industry), the record industry, and so on, it seems logical that the system should spread to the business of the publication and selling of books, under the financial control of vast organizations whose managers know about mass-merchandising techniques. It's not that the managers of conglomerates controlling the publishing divisions practice those techniques themselves but that they tend to *understand* the commercial power that these techniques can produce. The actual day-to-day activities of their acquired publishing houses are at some distance from those conglomerate overseers. The overseers of the diverse businesses merged into their corporate enterprises tend to have little emotional connection with "the product." Their real interest is primarily technical; it is in efficiency, the bottom line, rather than in details of the content of "the product." This remoteness may account in part for the lack of corporate pressures on the publishing houses they own concerning, for example, the political content of the books published. But they are likely to remain equally remote from the commitment to ideas and the nurturing of the best in literature which were the hallmark of the best of the independent book publishers. (One recalls the painful spectacle of the house of Knopf, once merged in good faith with Random House, then bought, along with Random House, by RCA, and then, along with the other divisions of Random House, unsentimentally put on the block by a bottom-line-minded RCA management and left dangling in limbo for about half a year, until the whole publishing complex was picked up by the Newhouse newspaper interests.) The managers of conglomerates controlling publishing houses are there to insure the constant elevation of annual net profits, and they have greater rapport with hard-nosed mass-merchandising techniques than with the muse. All those considerations have their place in supporting the unrestrained reign of hype, with its seemingly irresistible attraction for opportunistic and big-money writers, and its eerie capacity for luring and ensnaring unwary artists and for turning them, often against their better judgment, into travelling salesmen and TV pitchmen, and even causing some of them to make foolish talk, in television appearances, about their contributions to the free flow of ideas. The kind of emotional remoteness from "the product" which one senses in the conglomerates' central-management people now seems to be communicating itself to the people who are directly in charge of the publishing houses owned by the conglomerates, and more and more it seems that books are being regarded as interchangeable products somehow possessing, because of the manner of their promotion, a strange sort of uniformity. What is particularly striking to me about the frantic mass-merchandising and big-book promotions is the *undifferentiated* quality of what is being hawked once those books not singled out as potentially big money-makers have been, in effect, thrown into the discard. After all, some good books written by talented artists also sell well. But the nature of hype is really to obscure such distinctions. The books that are put out by the existing machine in hardcover and paperback may include works that are brilliant, works that are banal, and works that are miserably written, but they all tend to be inflated to approximately equal pressure, equal dimensions, by the hot air of hype—they all are made to seem strangely alike. Take any one—it could be good, it could be bad, or, as one woman in Hollywood who knows the publishing business put it to me, "it could be a pair of shoes." It's all treated as "product." And that is so because the mass merchandising, the hype, the frenzied pursuit of Number One which the book-publishing industry has turned to as a central and universal tool is in its very essence anti-art, and even anti-thought.

CHAPTER **15**

Banking On
Show Business

Someone who is standing near the heart of
conglomerate involvement in the book industry but is neither a professional writer nor a publisher nor a conglomerate
manager might naturally view all these developments in a
different light. Felix Rohatyn, of Lazard Frères, is such a
man. A month or so after the auction of the paperback rights
to *Princess Daisy,* I called on Rohatyn at the office of Lazard Frères, in Rockefeller Center. Lazard Frères is the
force that has been responsible for bringing together the
interested parties and mediating or negotiating the basic
conditions of a number of the biggest mergers of publishing
companies into conglomerate or big communications-busi-
ness organizations over the past twenty years or so—deals
such as the acquisition of Random House by RCA (and its
recent resale to the Newhouse interests), the Viking-Penguin merger, and the acquisition of the Book-of-the-Month
Club by Time, Inc. In many of those big deals, Rohatyn—
who, in addition to the position he occupies at Lazard
Frères as a senior partner, is a director of I.T.&T. and the
chairman of the New York Municipal Assistance Corporation—has been a central figure, and not necessarily in the
role of a mere passive broker. In an age of huge corporate

194

mergers and acquisitions, Rohatyn is recognized in the world of big corporations as someone who knows the workings of Wall Street inside out, who knows where the money and the power lie, and who is in a position to advise the parties to possible deals who can get what, and when and how, to best advantage. In a way, I think of Rohatyn as resembling the Hollywood dealmakers I have encountered—the packaging specialists who talk about "the spontaneous generation of a literary property." But while these people are putters-together of scriptwriters and such "elements" as actors, directors, and producers, and do fancy fiddling with TV- and paperback-tie-in rights, the kind of "spontaneous generation" that a Rohatyn engages in concerns "literary properties" representing not mere bits of film, film scripts, and their rights and subrights, but, rather, entire publishing entities, including their directors, staffs, and backlists (which are the artistic and intellectual inheritance of the whole course of the publishing houses' existence), and also all the contracts that their current and past authors have ever entered into with them, and what he generates is whole new corporate combinations involving those entities. There's nothing in the least bit immoral about this, of course, from the point of view either of the corporations involved or of the dealmaker himself. It's just part of the dynamics of the corporate market. Rohatyn himself is a man of culture, a reader in several languages on a very wide variety of literary as well as technical and professional subjects.

My interview with Rohatyn began with a discussion of the background of many of the original publishing mergers; namely, the need for the founders of family-owned independent publishing houses to exercise foresight in order to keep their companies from being broken up because of estate-settling problems. Then Rohatyn said that a big emerging issue in the publishing industry is "the cost of doing business, and the prices, which have been going out of sight, that have to be paid for literary properties." He continued, "It was one thing for Bantam to pay as much as a hundred thousand dollars for a book, but now it's paying a million, two million, three million, and the gambles now are just so great that the companies involved, unless they're very big companies, can't afford to take them."

When I asked him about the probable future of the merger trend in book publishing, he said, "I don't see this trend abating, necessarily, just because of the costs involved in doing business. Whether the companies themselves get together and form larger publishing conglomerates, on the order of McGraw-Hill, or whether they join up with a company like Time, Inc., the economic forces that make the business costlier and more heavily financed will go on, and therefore the requirement of size will continue."

I asked Rohatyn, concerning "the requirement of size," whether so-called economies of scale were considered a major factor in this continued concentration.

He said he thought not, since most publishing companies didn't own their own printing facilities. "It's the risk in buying rights that has become the big consideration," he went on. "When you have to plunk down three million dollars to buy the rights to a book of which you've read perhaps five chapters, you're rolling with very big dice." He indicated that the net effect was likely to be "further concentration or at least further agglomeration under one corporate roof."

I observed that the hoped-for cure—that is, further concentration in the publishing industry—seemed to me to be less a remedy than a part of the disease.

Rohatyn replied, "When these publishing companies become parts of larger companies, which can take bigger risks, they pay more for rights, and that brings the level of everything up to a different scale. It's a vicious circle. You talk about the notion of a cure. I don't think there is a cure. There isn't a cure for this situation any more than there is a way to operate a tiny automobile company today. But then I'm not sure that you have a disease. You have a situation that has changed."

I referred to the sense I had developed that the "situation that has changed" had caused substantial diversions of time and energy in the publishing industry from concentration on developing works of literary merit to such matters as auctions and the advance peddling of subsidiary rights.

Rohatyn replied, "I don't know the answer to that. It's a very serious question. Because I know how businesses work. And whatever businesses you're in, from the point of view of conglomerate management your attention is demanded by that area of the business where you have most at stake. And the stake is, increasingly, whether you're going to roll the dice for the latest novel by some woman living in Los Angeles who writes a thinly veiled account of scandals in the cosmetics industry; and when you have to decide whether you pay three million bucks for it, and hang all that out there in front of an unsuspecting public, while you may have a budding Faulkner trying to break through— I don't know whether he'll make it. My view is that he'll get the attention of somebody, but I don't know whether it'll be the right person. I think this: There's always a counterreaction. A trend always creates a countertrend. And the race to vulgarity that we've been involved in over the past fifteen or twenty years is going to create its own counterpressures, in the form of demands for quality, and for talent."

Concerning the supposed pressure that acquired publishing companies were subjected to from conglomerate headquarters, Rohatyn said he didn't himself have a sense "that you have a bunch of accountants descending on these people all the time." He went on, "The marketplace is more insidious than management. Look at the hoopla over that Henry Kissinger book when it was published, with television appearances and so forth. It's the dynamics of the marketplace at work. You can't fight that. Either you have to wait for the environment to change or you nurture new organisms that will cater to something different.''

Then he said, ''Everything in this world has turned into show business. Politics is show business. Running Chrysler is show business—look at Lee Iacocca trying to get the attention of Congress by running full-page ads in the newspapers. When I keep trying to keep New York City out of bankruptcy, there's a lot of show business involved. Sports is show business, and Henry Kissinger is show business, and when they popped two million dollars for his book they had to recoup it by throwing a big number on television, with his world-statesman posture and all the rest. You package all these things. That's the reality of the marketplace. And then you have this appetite for vulgarity, which seems limitless—as witness what the paperback houses are bidding millions of dollars for. Those are the realities of the marketplace. So, as I've said, everything in this world has turned into show business. And if you're not in show business, you're *really* off Broadway.''

INDEX